Teaching and Guiding
the Slow Learner

BAKER O. SHELTON

Parker Publishing Company, Inc.   West Nyack, N. Y.

PRINTED IN THE UNITED STATES OF AMERICA
ISBN—0-13-891325-0
B&P

Guidelines for Teachers and Counselors

As the students would have so aptly expressed it, Miss Smith, the tenth grade English teacher, had "blown her cool." Gertrude Smith, poised product of a sophisticated women's college, knew that something was *wrong*.

"You mean you have lost your book already?" she reproved. "But school only started last week. What could have happened to it?"

"I donno—somebody musta took it."

This was the third lost book. Today, four pupils came without pencils or notebooks. She was glad the final bell was due. Her head ached and she felt a trifle dizzy. Ignoring the muttered obscenity from the last row, she also closed her ears to the restless scraping of chairs, the furtive whispers and giggles. She dared not intercept the note being passed about.

Last week she had firmly expropriated a note, despite the expectant leers from the class. Steeling herself against shock, she had opened it. The crude filth of the cartoon had almost turned her stomach.

She suppressed a hysterical impulse to giggle. "Instead of taking *Major British Romantic Poets* in my junior year, I should have majored in beer, sex, cars and violence," she thought.

Gertrude Smith's intuition is correct. Something is critically wrong with our teaching if students have no interest in learning the material presented. That this sickness strikes deeper than the classroom is demonstrated by statistics from *Crime in the United States,* The FBI Uniform Crime Reports for 1969:

- Total arrests of youths under 15 were 517,250. A change of one-tenth of one percent from 1968.
- Total arrests of youths under 18 were 1,349,776, an increase of 3.7% over 1968.[1]
- That this surge in juvenile deliquency is not confined to the cities is further evidenced.
- Total suburban arrests under 18 were 342,949, an increase of 5.8% over 1968.[2]

Clearly, the nation faces a crisis for which schools must share part of the blame. The President's Commission on Law Enforcement states: "There is considerable evidence that some schools may have an indirect effect on deliquency by use of methods that create the conditions of failure for certain students. Mishandling by the school can lower the child's motivation to learn. It can aggravate his difficulties in accepting authority and generate or intensify hostility and alienation."[3]

Fortunately, public awareness is forcing education to concentrate funds and research on the problem. This book is designed to acquaint teachers, counselors and administrators with the results of these projects, as well as to publish the observations and experiences of the author during eight years of teaching and counseling slow learners. It offers theoretical models, practical advice, and successful programs. New materials and their sources are described and

---

[1] *Crime in the United States.* FBI Uniform Crime Reports 1969. Department of Justice. U.S. Government Printing Office. Washington, D.C. p. 112. Table 26.
[2] Ibid p. 130. Table 38.
[3] Task Force Report: Juvenile Deliquency and Youth Crime. The Presidents Commission on Law Enforcement and Administration of Justice. U.S. Government Printing Office. Washington, D.C. 1967 p 49.

suggestions advanced for improving present practices. *Teaching and Guiding the Slow Learner* is written from the viewpoint of teachers and counselors, because "that is where the action is!" They are well aware that the problem is not only technological, but has a highly emotional content that must be released.

Some educators will immediately challenge the title on the grounds that no such human as a "slow learner" exists. They maintain that only the methods used in teaching them are inappropriate. This question is not yet resolved. For practical purposes, this book will regard the term "slow learner" to include not only those who do not easily grasp abstractions and symbolizations, but also those students underachieving because of culturally-deprived backgrounds or severe, unresolved emotional problems.

BAKER O. SHELTON

Table of Contents

Chapter 2—Continued

**3 Initiating the Elementary School
Remedial Program**..................... 55

4 Teaching the Disadvantaged Child......... 79

Chapter 7—Continued

Teaching and Guiding
the Slow Learner

chapter 1

Understanding the Behavior of the Slow Learner

A teacher remarked recently, "My one period of slow learners is the most exasperating of the whole day. If I had to teach several classes like that I would quit."

Obviously, his attitude disqualified him to teach even that one period. Lacking in professional empathy for his handicapped charges, he could not have taught them much. It is common practice among teachers to label slow learners as lazy, obstinate, careless, vicious, ill-mannered, deceitful, mutinous, etc. Some of these terms do apply to certain individuals, yet basically, slow learners have the same needs, drives and emotions as other children. The difference lies beneath the façade of bravado and indifference. They are frightened, confused and bitter, having been made to feel inferior by comparison to their peers. That they have accepted this derogation is all too evident, but it is a most humiliating knowledge with which to live. The level of anxiety it generates is unacceptable. Necessary defenses must be erected to protect their egos from collapse, and maintaining these defenses requires energy that should have been poured into learning. Until you can recognize and understand these defenses, you are not prepared to teach them.

This chapter will explore the emotional life of the slow learner and explain his behavior. When you are ready to teach them you will find few guides or established techniques to aid you. Patience, humanity, and ingenuity are your resources. If you are not easily discouraged and are exhilarated by challenge, you will find it rewarding. Just remember, anyone can teach the so called "good kids."

DEFINING THE TERM "SLOW LEARNER"

This brings us immediately into the realm of semantics: "Slower than whom"?—"Slower in learning what"?

By using the curve of normal distribution to score tests we automatically create slow learners. If everyone could be made smarter by some scientific discovery, the same persons would still be slow learners since they would still fall below the mean of the population. The fault lies not in the tests, but in the invidious comparisons we make from them. A revision in our scale of human·values is badly needed to put education in proper perspective. Logically, since humans differ widely in all characteristics, failing to make an arbitrary score in algebra should be no more humiliating than failing to grow the usual number of wisdom teeth.

Most slow learners are slow only in certain academic processes requiring reading ability, abstract thinking, seeing relationships, and making generalizations. By contrast, the areas in which they are often successful span a large portion of our society. They become artists, musicians, athletes, business men, pool players, actors, and politicians. Once out of school, they cannot be selected out of the population. This raises the question as to whether the subjects we teach in school are those actually needed for success in life. Moreover, as far as personal adjustment is concerned, higher education provides no insurance against suicide, divorce, alcoholism, intolerance, or insanity.

It would seem that several questions pertaining to schools and education need to be researched thoroughly.

1. Is our curriculum out-dated and in need of drastic revision?
2. Are our teaching techniques those best designed for efficient learning?
3. How valid are the variables we have selected with which to measure success?

Since this book is intended to be practical and of immediate use to teachers, counselors, and administrators, the above questions will be left to researchers. Slow learners will be defined as *those students who fail to reach the average achievement of the majority of students in their age groups.*

WHAT MAKES THEM SLOW?

Slow learners differ from each other as much as the rest of the population and, in practice, must be dealt with as individuals rather than groups. Only for the purpose of recognition can they be divided roughly into several categories which often overlap:

1. Those with recognizable handicaps such as impaired sight, speech, or hearing or debilitating diseases requiring specialized treatment outside the class room.

2. The mentally retarded, who can be taught by teachers in schools with special education departments, providing the retardation is not too severe.

3. Those with special physiological disabilities about which little is known, such as dyslexia or inability to read, directionality or inability to establish left to right progression, poor visual perception or inability to recognize and interpret words or pictures. Some experts believe this is caused by immaturity.

4. The genuine slow learner, who can progress in school, but

cannot grasp higher abstractions and symbols and who only advances one-half to three-quarters of a grade per year. No one knows why this is so, but it is probably of genetic origin.

5. Those whose emotional problems originate with significant persons in their lives, but who use the school in an attempt to resolve these conflicts and whose anxiety level weakens or destroys their ability to concentrate.

6. Those whose cultural and social background has been so deprived as to make them poorly equipped for school and poorly motivated to learn.

Regardless of the source of their predicament, lack of success soon compounds their problems. No matter how it is glossed over, failure in our competitive society bears the stigma of inferiority. Unless this is corrected quickly, slow learners become failure oriented. Once this role is accepted, they pile failure upon failure until only a miracle can reverse the regression of their school experience.

THEIR FIRST ENCOUNTER WITH FAILURE

Every individual looks at the world through his own unique window. The view he sees is interpreted and translated into meaning to match his own peculiar experiences. If he fails in his first few encounters with school, he will expect to fail throughout school. Preschool children, unless severely handicapped or retarded, are not overly-concerned with their failures. They have not yet been graded on their performance by adults and compared with each other. Since adults attach little significance to play, children take their cue from this attitude and exhibit only slight emotional involvement with their triumphs or defeats. All this changes with school. The child has now embarked on the journey which will eventually determine his placement in society. The prestige of the parent and teacher are now involved. The child is soon made aware of the value adults place on his performance. He is exhorted to "study hard and make good grades." If he does so, he is rewarded with smiles and praise. If he does not, he is greeted with frowns, sharp questions, and reprimands. If this is unsuccessful in raising his grade, the pressure increases and he may be punished. It does not take long for him to realize that he has done something which the significant persons in his life deem "bad." He may be puzzled and bewildered by this at first, but if he has self-confidence and ability, he sets about correcting his mistakes and learning to do the tasks that result in praise and approval. However, if he lacks ability to match the performance of his peers, or cannot grasp by himself the requirements of the situation, he soon becomes frightened, confused, and resentful.

It should be noted, at this point, that there exists a different group of children who are also in deep trouble not described by this pattern. They come from homes where the parents themselves have not had a successful school experience and who place little value on their children's achievement. They often heap scorn upon scholastic success, and their children, mimicking the parent's attitude, make little effort to excell.

Regardless of the cause of failure, this is the point at which the school must intervene or lose the struggle. It may be in the first grade, or it may be as late as the fourth, but at whatever stage it occurs, the failure is critical. If the student can be helped over this hurdle, his confidence may be restored and satisfactory progress resumed. If he continues to fail, his self esteem suffers progressive deterioration and he comes to accept himself as inferior. Schooling becomes a punishing experience and he hates it. Teachers and principals are no longer friends but oppressors. Curiosity and desire to learn are consumed by bitterness, and a steady decline is almost assured.

Failure feeds upon itself. Once he starts to regress, he falls behind his classmates. New input has no significance for him since he has not learned the fundamentals which were to prepare him for it. Gradually he loses the skills necessary to compete with his peers. He will soon be issued a text he cannot read or asked to learn fractions without knowing how to divide. Fearing now to demonstrate his lack of ability to the class and teacher, he sullenly refuses to participate in class work. Dreading to be handed back a paper with a large red F in the upper right hand corner, he neglects to turn in homework or test papers. In order to justify this omission, both to himself and to the teacher, he forgets his pencil or loses his text book. He selects the last seat in the last row in hopes of escaping attention, and, as a result, has an excuse for not hearing assignments or seeing the board clearly. Not understanding what the teacher is talking about, his mind wanders. Soon he is mercifully asleep and temporarily out of his misery.

The stage is now set for the final act of the tragedy—the self-fulfilling prophecy. The feedback he receives from his environment tells him he is retarded. This role he accepts. He begins to trust all messages which corroborate this brutal illusion and screen out all messages that conflict with it. From now on, no one will be able to convince him he is not "dumb."

RECOGNIZING THE DEFENSES SLOW LEARNERS ERECT

We all need to respect ourselves and to feel respected. To do this we need the approval of the people important to us, which, in the case of students, are parents, teachers, and fellow-students. If we think they do not approve of us, we feel cheap in their eyes; stress builds up, and we make unconscious attempts to reduce it. These attempts are the defenses the failure begins to erect to protect his ego. Just how they operate is not clear, but it is easy to discern that different types of personalities erect different defenses. The selection appears to be on a subconscious level and is aimed at reducing tension and anxiety.

Dr. James C. Coleman, at the University of California states: "When frustration continues, or the individual is confronted with a succession of frustrating situations stemming from the same source, anger gradually blends into hostility. In a general sense, hostility may be viewed as prolonged anger. It involves increased drive toward destruction, damage or hurt to the object viewed as the source of frustration."[1]

Some failures, therefore, become hostile and aggressive. They appear to be attempting to change their environment by direct assult upon it. They are deliberately disobedient and belligerent, resorting at times to violence against school personnel and property. Obscenity, bullying and cheating are their means of demonstrating contempt. They are raucous and scornful of education and school regulations, adopting bizarre dress and hair styles. They flaunt their disdain of educational values with alcoholism and drug abuse. It is not difficult to see how this total rejection of their environment compensates for lack of success. If a thing has no value, one need put forth no effort to obtain it. But this is an over-simplification. Psychologists call it "acting-out." These children are really reducing the anxiety aroused by taboo impulses by allowing these impulses to surface.

Others conceal hostility by adopting the opposite tactic of withdrawal. They deliberately do nothing, skip classes, and become truant. They can assure themselves that they have not failed because they have not tried.

Defense mechanisms are as varied as the individuals who adopt them. Some feign illness, missing school from

[1] Coleman, James C. *Abnormal Psychology and Modern Life.* Chicago, Illinois: Scott Foresman and Company. Third edition, 1964, p 92.

deceptively authentic complaints that pack the clinic. If forced to attend class, they are dull and apathetic and sleep whenever possible. They can console themselves with the thought that an invalid like themselves could not be expected to do hard work.

One of the most infuriating to teachers is the game of "faking out the establishment." Bright students, using the school to frustrate their parent's wishes, are often adept at this tactic. It consists of a bland and cooperative attitude that produces nothing. They usually have a multitude of apparently plausible excuses for failure. They turn in well-executed papers on the wrong topic. They deliberately misunderstand directions, studying erroneous assignments. They obfuscate answers to tests with witty irrelevancies. They plan and cooperate in cunning maneuvers to outwit the principal. The knowledge that they can outwit adults apparently compensates them for the failure they have deliberately brought upon themselves.

Every teacher is acquainted with the clown. He is a pitiful figure to both teachers and students, having sacrificed his dignity as a human being for the attention his distractions generate.

Undersized boys often regress to an earlier stage of maturity and become childish, thus hoping to lower the standards expected of them.

Children of tyrannical parents displace the hostility they dare not show at home onto substitute authority figures such as teachers. This also takes the form of scapegoating weaker students. Dropouts are, on the whole, particularly intolerant of other races and of each other. Sensitive to the slightest condescension, they deride themselves continually, thus taking the sting out of anticipated devaluation from others.

Girls seem less sensitive to school failure than boys, but when there is a complicating home condition, they choose extreme withdrawal or a sort of emotional insulation. Their primary defense seems to be sex. They begin to dress and act seductively, deliberately attracting the attention of males. This successful use of a biological asset apparently draws attention away from their school failure.

There is a great deal of overlap in these defenses, and, since failures cannot long fool themselves, feedback alerts them to the need for stronger and more expensive protectors. Anxiety floods them anew and must be drained off by impulsive, and often, random actions. Concentration or motivation can find no place in the mind of a tense and jittery child.

During the three years the author spent as director of a program for potential dropouts, a daily diary was kept, recording observations and impressions. The following are excerpts from that diary. Many of the defenses previously described can be recognized in action. It should be noted here that most of these students were suffering from severe emotional problems not always characteristic of genuine slow learners. Where the school possesses the facilities, the relatively well-adjusted slow learner should be separated from the emotionally disturbed.

> They cannot stay quiet . . . they must move about, laughing, talking, whistling—indulging in horseplay . . . talk must be loud—actions rough—they continually react with each other.
>
> They continually deride themselves and each other—their favorite term for themselves is "retards" . . . it is not good-natured banter . . . quarrels and fights start easily but quickly cool off . . . scapegoating is common.
>
> Their attention span is from five to ten minutes . . . no tests we have given them are valid, because after the first three or four questions, they lose interest and mark answers at random . . . the same is true of programmed instruction.
>
> They demonstrate independence of teachers and speakers by putting feet on desks, walking about, looking out the window, or challenging statements pointlessly . .

they must preserve independence with some gesture, no matter how weak.

They complain endlessly . . . school is boring . . . teachers have it in for them . . . what they are taught is useless . . . Some of this is true but they must put the blame on someone else.

Rough humor or obscenity relieves tension when they are faced with a threatening situation or something they do not understand.

Everything must be locked up or bolted down . . . anything loose disappears . . . since they never bring papers or pencils these must be furnished but carefully accounted for after each class—they never return them.

Intense rage can be aroused over trifles . . . some seem to fill up with impounded anger like a bottle until they overflow. The result is often smashed furniture or broken windows. . . . for several weeks after such an outburst they are quite docile.

When you preach to them or nag them, they tune you out.

They have almost no sense of right or wrong . . . the clever ones are usually one step ahead of the law.

About a third show signs of illness, being especially susceptible to colds and sniffles.

They are almost all untidy in dress, personal appearance and hygiene . . . even those from apparently good homes . . . this appears to be a gesture of defiance aimed at middle-class school and social values.

Their personal lives are poorly organized, usually pretty dull in spite of frequent skirmishes with the law.

They keep late hours and usually spend much time sleeping in class . . . this also is a form of escapism.

Attendance is poor but they do little but hang around when they stay out . . . they often return to school after hours . . . they hate it, but it still holds an attraction for them.

Their fear of condescension is one of the greatest hurdles to helping them . . . We had to issue regular text books for them to carry about just for appearance . . . these were never used.

Lest the foregoing appear too grim and discouraging, a lighter note needs to be added. A sizeable number of these in the project managed by hook or crook to be graduated. A few are even attending college. This is the brighter side and worth all the discouragement you have experienced.

The following true account of Janet illustrates the terminal state of an emotionally-disturbed slow learner who failed to receive help in the crucial period of her education.

Janet appeared almost mysteriously in the high school guidance office six weeks after school began. The secretary noticed her sitting unobtrusively in the reception room and asked her why she was there. Janet replied that she had come to register. When queried about the name of the school she had attended, Janet confessed that she had not been in school at all this year. At that point she was referred to a counselor.

Huddled into a shabby coat several sizes too large, Janet replied tonelessly to the counselor's questions.

"I'm sixteen."

"Why haven't you registered before? You've missed quite a lot of school."

She shrugged.

He tried another tack. "Where did you go to school last year."

"In Salem."

"What grade were you in?"

Her response was delayed, as though remembering were difficult. "I don't know—I think it was the eighth grade."

"Did you pass the eighth grade?"

"I don't know."

By this time the counselor realized he had a problem on his hands. He studied her sad face, her long, uncombed, blond hair, the ugly run in her hose. At last he asked softly, "Why did you decide to register today?"

She shrank back in her chair and her voice was ashamed. "My father—he was drunk—he chased me out of the house."

The counselor enrolled Janet in the ninth grade and

sent a social worker to Janet's home. This disclosed that Janet's father was a construction worker who moved about wherever there was employment. He seldom worked but a few weeks on a job because of alcoholism. Her mother was employed occasionally as a waitress but was too weak to provide a stable home. Two years previous, an older sister had disappeared from the house and had not been heard from since.

From the beginning, Janet's school performance was dismal. She left her books in her locker and sat through classes with no participation. Without excuse she missed several days a week. The counselor tried to hold regular counseling sessions with her but could make no contact. She was not hostile, simply noncommunicative. Her mind seemed empty. He arranged a referral to the Guidance Clinic where she was enrolled in a therapy group, but after the second meeting she stopped attending. He found her a job after school, but she failed to show up for work after the first week.

At this writing, she is still enrolled in the ninth grade and occasionally attends. Teachers estimate she reads at the fourth grade level and knows almost no arithmetic. They feel her attendance is beneficial, showing she is still in contact with reality. They and the counselor know they should somehow build up her ego strength, but they don't know how—even worse—they don't know anyone who does.

UNDERSTANDING THE EMOTIONAL CONTENT OF THEIR SCHOOL AND COMMUNITY RELATIONS

That the behavior described in the preceding paragraphs operates on a subconscious level accounts for its irrationality. Its source is emotional rather than cognitive, and is, therefore, impervious to logic and reasoning. This also explains the ineffectiveness of counseling and other social services offered by churches and welfare agencies. Teachers and principals, too often discouraged and offended by the apparent rejection of their sincere efforts, ascribe the behavior of the slow learner to mere stubbornness and abandon him to a "well-deserved fate." The explanation, however, is not that simple. Their conduct is triggered by anxiety, and, in many ways, resembles the experimental neurosis induced in laboratory rats by continuous discrepancy between their capacity to learn and the requirements of the situation. Moreover, the vast difference between slow learners' real selves (failures) and their ideal selves (respected students) generates inner conflict and confuses their self-identity. Under such stress for long periods of time, it is small wonder they not only lack insight but resent having their contradictions pointed out to them.

Rejected by the real world, they retreat gradually into fantasy. Their reactions become less and less adaptive, since they are not reacting to reality but to their interpretation of it. No longer capable of discriminating behavior, they become steadily more rigid in response. Year after year this distortion of reality grows until it obscures all else. Violence and hate become the props with which they maintain their self-respect and prevent collapse of their egos. At this stage they are dangerous, focusing their impounded rage upon school and society. Having reached it, there is small hope for their rehabilitation.

WHY THEY FINALLY DROP OUT

Although people differ as to how much stress they can resist, everyone reaches a point at which some action must be taken to escape. We often endure a long series of frustrations only to errupt at something trivial. Moreover, psychologists tell us that the longer we endure stress the more severe it becomes. Dropouts have been weakened by psychic injuries until they are vulnerable even to insignificant annoyances.

This is the reason the excuses they give for dropping out of school are often petty. They rationalize their actions with childish sophistry.

"I feel not wanted." (often in spite of valiant efforts to retain them.)

"I do not need an education." (although they cannot find a job without it.)

"My family needs my support." (although they earn little or nothing.)

"Teachers should be more considerate." (although they show little consideration for anyone.)

"What I am taught is useless." (although employers demand it.)

The true reason for dropping out is humiliation beyond human endurance. Put yourself in their place. Suppose that for years you have been given a note to take to your family at regular intervals stating that your work was unsatisfactory or failing. How long would you stay after you could legally escape? When viewed in this context, dropping out is not as irrational as it appears.

chapter 2

Developing a Practical Concept for Teaching Slow Learners

Many studies have been made of slow learners, many projects designed and many voices raised in advice, some of it excellent; but all have been on a relatively limited scale. No specifics could cover all slow learners from differing geographical, ethnic, and environmental backgrounds, yet no school system, as far as known, has attempted a coordinated program from preschool to the twelfth grade. If the problem is ever to be solved, it must be done on a continuing basis that guarantees the slow learner a complete, satisfying educational experience through steady growth at his own pace. Using him as a guinea pig and then tossing him back into the meat grinder only serves to bewilder and embitter him all the more.

Since it is impossible to develop a methodology that would meet all contingencies, the individual educator is thrown back on his own resources. What is needed is a series of broad, practical concepts based on common sense and experience to serve as a guide for teachers, counselors and administrators. This chapter will attempt to develop sound, empirical principles which, when seriously applied, will prove helpful.

TEACHING YOURSELF FIRST

Since theorists differ and research is contradictory, the only practical procedure for an educator in the field is to teach himself first. No substitute exists for getting your feet wet, but a prior study will prevent initial disillusionment and discouragement. The first practical suggestion is to read a number of excellent publications. The following are recommended:

School Dropouts: Summary 1967–S1. Research Division, National Education Association. Washington, D.C.

CAMP (Concepts and Applications of Mathematics Project) Project Conference Report. Dr. Paul C Rosenbloom, Director, Central College, Pella, Iowa.

The Educationally Retarded and Disadvantaged. The Sixty-sixth Yearbook of the National Society for the Study of Education, 1967. University of Chicago Press. Chicago, Ill.

The Low Achiever in Mathematics. U.S. Department of Health Education and Welfare. OE 29061. 1965. U.S. Government Printing Office. Washington, D.C.

Reading is not sufficient. You need to see for yourself. Visit classes of slow learners and talk with the instructors. Above all, visit the communities where the disadvantaged live. When you have done these things, you are ready to tackle the problem.

What are the frustrations of the slow learner?

1. Either the assignments given him are too difficult or he has fallen too far behind his grade level to understand and perform the tasks required of him.
2. He lacks motivation to learn, either because his background has been too deprived, his home-induced emo-

tional problems are too severe, or his learning attempts have received no suitable encouragement or reinforce ment.

3. He has become failure oriented because of repeated defeats and thus no longer believes himself capable of learning.
4. The material he is assigned has not been made meaningful to him, so he sees little purpose in learning it.
5. He is flooded with anxiety produced by the defenses he has erected against self-devaluation.
6. He is bitter and hostile toward school and society because of the humiliation he has suffered.

The cure to the slow learner's frustrations is to devise remedies for each of these maladies.

APPLYING LEARNING THEORY TO THEIR PROBLEMS

Fortunately, discoveries in learning theory both new and old supply some of the answers.

Initially, how much the pupil knows must be discovered in order to start him at a level at which he can be successful. This can be determined roughly by achievement tests and teacher's diagnostic measures. A number of these are named and discussed in Chapter 3. Since many slow learners will not apply themselves enough to achievement tests to make the results valid, some inducement may be necessary. Students may be given the day off as a reward for satisfactory performance, or, if this is not practical, some type of refreshments can be served or other privileges granted after the test's completion. If at all possible, it is best to test them alone, or at least widely separated from each other, so as to avoid the interactions which they cannot resist.

Starting a pupil at the point his test indicates is not always an easy matter. It may require his separation from his classmates which results in resentment and adds to his feeling of inferiority. Nongraded classes, where they exist, are a partial solution. Other devices are available and will be discussed in later chapters. At any rate, much tact must be exercised at this point in order not to lose him again.

A second difficult decision is the nature of the material supplied to him. He may be reading at such a low level that the only available instructional matter is far below his maturity. A ninth grader, reading at the third or fourth grade level, will be insulted by an elementary school reader. Negro children will be rightfully scornful of the polite, well-dressed, suburban moppets so often found in texts. Easy reading material at appropriate maturity levels is coming on the market and will be identified in later chapters.

A third major hurdle is his indifference. He is not a self-starter and needs much individual supervision, prodding, and explanation to get him off dead center. This tutoring can be performed by teacher's aides, or by older students.

No matter how difficult, it is fundamental that he be given an assignment at which he can be successful. Nothing will start him back to work except success. Once he does take hold, he must be rewarded for his efforts, no matter how small, as long as they are in the desired direction. In very difficult cases, extrinsic rewards, such as candy, drinks, and special privileges may be necessary, yet a smile and a compliment in front of his classmates will work wonders. Immediate knowledge of his success must also be available to him. Nothing is as rewarding, even to hard-core dropouts, as the realization that he can learn like other students.

How do we reward him? How do we prove to him he is successful? The universal emolument that schools dispense is grades. Under the present competitive grading system, slow learners are deprived of this reward. Actually, it is reserved only for the upper quartile students. They are truly the school's privileged class. Only A's and B's are actually reinforcing. They can be traded for such desirable baubles as the approval of teachers, praise from parents, envy of peers. They can be cashed for honor roll lists, student offices, college admissions, lucrative job offers. On the contrary, what college sends its admission representative to interview an average student? What parent proudly exhibits to his friends a report card with a dreary row of C's? As for D's and F's—they are actually punishing. If slow learners are to be kept working at school tasks, they must be able to share in the rewards. Lacking the ability to match the achievement of their peers, they deserve to be graded on their effort. Progress from their starting point deserves a C, good progress deserves a B, excellent progress deserves an A. Contrary to the headshakings of many teachers, where this has been introduced, it has had little repercussion on the school at large, while the effect on slow learners has been notable.

Progress grading is nothing new as far as schools are concerned. Objection to it is largely based on the claim that it dilutes standards and fails to show a true picture of what the student has learned to parents, colleges and employers. This claim is no longer valid. Grades are so subjective as to be almost meaningless. Standards vary from teacher to teacher, school to school and locality to locality. The blossoming of new courses has produced a crop of alphabetical names that no longer identify the subject or the content. Grades are now (and probably always were) what the individual teacher makes them. In a recent contest at the author's school ten unidentified English papers were given to five English teachers to rate. There was so little agreement that the same paper received both the highest and lowest rating from different teachers. Not long ago, due to a hardship caused by changing schools, a student, in order to graduate, was allowed to take eleventh and twelfth grade English at the same time. You must have already guessed the denouement. He passed twelfth grade English and failed eleventh grade. The teacher made the difference.

Assuming that a slow learner has been started at the

point at which he can succeed, has been provided material suitable to his academic and maturity level, and has been reinforced for his progress with appropriate grades, the teacher's next step brings into play a number of recognized learning principles.

1. He must be taught in simple steps that he can master at his own pace. In-put overload can only result in selective retention and frustration.
2. He must receive immediate reinforcement for any success. This is necessary to insure repetition of his successful behavior.
3. He must receive a variety of stimulation, since all children do not learn in the same fashion or by the same means.
4. The material must be made meaningful to him to insure retention.
5. He must be provided with immediate knowledge of the result of his work. If not, he has no feedback to guide further activity.
6. He must be given the opportunity to practice his knowledge and skills through distributed repetition and a variety of appropriate tasks.
7. His primary instruction at every level must be initiated through careful priming, and then painstakingly shaped by increasingly accurate corrections which are reinforced.

B.F. Skinner of Harvard University, best known as the chief exponent of operant conditioning, covers many of these principles in his book *The Technology of Teaching.* He maintains (and this is obvious to thoughtful and troubled teachers) that schools still depend to a large extent on aversive control to shape learning. They punish mistakes, thus teaching what *not* to do. A wrong answer results in a frown, public correction, or a poor grade. This is negative reinforcement. It *does* teach the student what is incorrect but not what is correct. It is more likely to lead to successive wrong answers in a trial-and-error effort to find the right one. The mildest criticism that can be made for this type of teaching is that it is inefficient. For slow learners it is disastrous. The anxiety it generates through frustration soon results in diminishing attempts to learn and final abandonment. If, instead, a contingency is provided whereby the correct answer is discovered first and then reinforced, the same behavior is most likely to occur again. This is the purpose of programmed instruction, and in speaking of it, Dr. Skinner states: "Special techniques have been designed to arrange what are called contingencies of reinforcement— the relations which prevail between behavior on the one hand and the consequences of that behavior on the other, with the result that a more effective control of behavior has been achieved." He continues: "Once we have arranged the particular type of consequence called a reinforcement, our techniques permit us to shape the behavior of an organism almost at will."[1]

Products of Dr. Skinner's principles are programmed instruction and the teaching machine. Both are useful in teaching slow learners. By themselves, however, they are merely gadgets. They must be integrated into the classroom by a resourceful teacher.

To clarify the seven previously outlined learning principles, we will take them up one at a time and illustrate how each can be used.

The first states that he must be taught in simple steps which he can master at his own pace. Programmed instruction, providing it is available and the student can read, does advance in small, simple steps which build upon each other. The student cannot proceed to the next step until he has made the correct response to the one on which he is working. Reaching the correct response, he is immediately reinforced by the knowledge of his success. He need not wait until the teacher corrects his paper and returns it the following day—or the following week. He need not sit through the

---

[1] Skinner, B.F. *The Technology of Teaching.* New York. Appleton, Century, Crofts. 1968 pp 8-9.

questions of a dozen other children waiting to ask his own and dreading, when he does, to make a fool of himself. With programmed instruction he does not fear exposure of his inadequacy, since he works in privacy and can travel at his own pace. By successive correct answers, his learning is shaped to any desired degree, almost without his realizing it. There are no incorrect responses to be extinguished. Although this may not be desirable for all students, for slow learners it provides needed mastery of fundamentals. No longer need the slow learner reach high school without knowing how to divide or how to construct a simple sentence. He enjoys only success so that the destructive effects of failure are avoided. Where programmed instruction is not available, a tape recorder and mimeographed response sheets using the same principles can be employed.

The second principle is to provide reinforcement or reward for learning (if school system permits). This is not new and has been used by industry and government for years. Employees who take additional courses in school or learn new skills are promoted or receive pay increases. It is not surprising that it is effective with children. The only difference is that for children the reward must be immediate and meaningful. Since slow learners are usually "thing and now" oriented, promises for the future and deferred rewards are not effective.

A number of studies of the effect of rewards on learning have demonstrated its capabilities. Martin J. Higgins, Director of Research, West Chester State College, and Sidney Archer, Director of the Eastern Regional Institute for Education, Syracuse, New York, report on an experiment in which both lower socioeconomic and upper socioeconomic pupils were divided into groups, one set to receive conventional rewards such as praise, grades, etc.; the other set to receive extrinsic rewards consisting of a bus ride on school time to a motion picture theatre where refreshments would be served. The task required of them was to improve their performance on an achievement test over that of their previous grade level. The results showed that the lower socio-economic group who received the extrinsic reward performed better than their counterparts at a significant level of confidence. This was not true of the upper socioeconomic groups. This led the authors to conclude:

A. "Lower socioeconomic students can do significantly better in testing situations if the rewards for doing so are meaningful."

B. "The intrinsic, or conventional rewards, of our present public schools are not very meaningful to lower socioeconomic students."[2]

The third principle is that of providing a variety of stimulation by the use of multi-sensory learning devices such as cassettes and records combined with overhead projectors using color transparencies, or writing assignments combined with recordings or films. There is a growing accumulation of evidence about children that each has his own best method of learning. Slow learners, in particular, need all the help they can obtain through different sensory input. Modern classroom techniques provide sight, sound, and tactile stimulation through the use of overhead projectors, color transparencies, films, film strips, drill tapes, machines that guide reading and word recognition, television, and mockups.

One outstanding handicap, characteristic of slow learners, is their reading retardation. This may have many causes, but one factor appears to be the prevalence of pictures and sound in their lives. They have been raised with television, motion pictures, comic books, and picture magazines. Counselors have long noted that on the nationally-used STEP achievement tests, students with low reading scores often

---

[2] Higgins, Martin J. and Archer, N. Sidney. "Interaction Effect of Extrinsic Rewards and Socio-economic Strata." *Personnel and Guidance Journal.* December 1968. Vol 47 No. 4. p 318.

have good listening scores. They have learned to learn by hearing.

Slow learners are also more easily taught by imitation. Mock-ups, simulations, and visual aids that can be manipulated are highly effective. This raises the possibility that all classrooms for slow learners should be laboratories similar to the math laboratories now being adopted in many schools.

The fourth principle, that learning must be made meaningful, requires considerable ingenuity on the part of the teacher. Its effectiveness is demonstrated by the following experiment reported by Herbert Klausmeier of the University of Wisconsin. Klausmeier and Feldhusen worked with three groups of children at a mean age of 127 months. One group had IQ's of 56-81, another group had IQ's of 90-110, and the high group IQ's of 120-146. Each child was taught to count or to add using exercises of difficulty appropriate to his intelligence level. The tasks to be learned were socially significant and each child was taught as meaningfully as possible. There was no significant difference among the three groups in amount of recall at five minutes or six weeks after the original learning. In other words, slow learners taught at an appropriate level of difficulty and as meaningfully as possible retained the learning as well as children with greater ability.[3]

Making instruction meaningful can be defined as making it relate to something the student is familiar with— something in his daily life. For example, the Math Curriculum Guide of the Stockton Unified School District, Stockton, California, suggests the following mathematics exercises which were contributed by nearby business firms on their own letterheads. These were practical problems encountered daily in business.

---

[3] Klausmeier, Herbert. "Psychological Research and Classroom Learning". *New Dimensions in Learning.* Association for Supervision and Curriculum Development: NEA Washington, D.C. 1962. p 70.

LESSON #3

Sears Roebuck and Co.
Change cents to proper fractions

LESSON #9

Pacific Gas and Electric Co.
Convert decimal equivalents to improper fractions

LESSON #5

Valley Lumber and Supply Co.
Convert feet to inches and inches to feet[4]

During a recent summer institute, in which the author took part, English and social studies were taught from the daily newspaper. Household kitchens and back yards furnished material for science. Sports and auto racing supplied math problems. Full length films presented literature in an understandable form in the classroom, and industrial films, furnished free, related education to job holding. Schools are only beginning to take lessons out of the confines of hard covers and into the student's world.

Anthropologists tell us that primitive peoples initiate children directly into adult culture. Almost from infancy, children begin to learn the duties they will be expected to perform as adults. Their learning is meaningful to them, and they are eager to master it. By contrast, we keep our children insulated from real life until they are almost grown. What they are required to learn seems to have little relevance to their lives. Convince yourself. Take a poll of your students. They will tell you school bores them. This applies to good students—bad students—indifferent students alike. Counselors have long noted the phenomenon that an incredible number of high school students do not know what their fathers do to earn a living.

---

[4] Math Curriculum Guide. California State Department of Education. Office of Compensatory Education. The Stockton Unified School District. Stockton, California.

Much has been said recently about heuristic teaching (encouraging the student to discover principles and relationships for himself). With the well-motivated student it is highly effective, but the slow learner tunes it out. Why? Because it implies curiosity—the desire to explore—to master new concepts. These instincts, natural to childhood, have long been extinguished in slow learners by a succession of bitter defeats. It takes a skillful teacher to once again make learning meaningful to them. An excellent formula for such teaching is to be found in the Biological Sciences Curriculum Course using Special Materials.[5] The Teacher's Handbook outlines the following procedures:

1. Lessons should be carefully planned in sequential form.
2. Lessons should be kept flexible, but students and teacher should determine their starting point and direction.
3. Classroom studies should be related to the student's own experience.
4. All students can learn.
5. The ability of some students has been untapped.
6. Learning takes place best under conditions that encourage curiosity and involvement of students in all phases of the program including planning.
7. The attitude of the teacher is of greatest importance. *Learning is best accomplished if the teacher is also learning.*

The fifth learning principle relates to the necessity for students to receive immediate knowledge of their work. There can be no doubt that this is important in maintaining interest. Any golfer knows the thrill of watching the results of his swing as a good drive arcs straight and high from the tee. It is doubtful if many would play at all if they were not allowed to see how close their iron shot came to the pin. In a class of thirty students, teachers can seldom grade all papers and cover every problem assigned. If they manage to do so, it

_____
[5] Teachers Handbook. Biological Science: Patterns and Processes. Biological Sciences Curriculum Study. Holt, Reinhart and Winston, Inc. New York, N.Y. 1964 p XIV.

is long after the student performed the actual work, and by that time, feedback effect has been lost. Even worse, teachers often assign a grade to the entire paper, as in the case of themes, or simply mark an answer wrong without explaining the error in detail. It is safe to say that no learning takes place under these circumstances. The slow learner in particular needs the reinforcement of immediate knowledge of success if he is to continue working. He is in a deprived state where praise is concerned as surely as the laboratory animal who has not been fed, and this is the situation psychologists claim necessary for behavior to be shaped by reinforcement. If teacher aides are assigned in sufficient ratio so that slow learners receive constant assistance, a manifest change takes place. Even the most hardened individual secretly enjoys being told, "That's very good."

Teaching machines with programmed instruction automatically supply immediate knowledge of results and are therefore reinforcing. They are well suited to teaching slow learners, but no machine can entirely replace the genuine interest and approval of another human being.

The sixth principle, that the learner must be given the opportunity to absorb, integrate, and retain his new knowledge through repetition and distributed practice is generally well known in schools, but not so generally well practiced. Repetition and practice, as such, are boring to both good and bad students alike, and they shirk it whenever possible. Slow learners, with short attention spans, are particularly averse to drill. They can be taught the multiplication tables every year for six years and yet arrive at the ninth grade without knowing them. This is because they never really learned them in the first place. Teachers of thirty pupils cannot supervise each individual and must content themselves with making assignments and hoping for the best.

Research has shown that more retention is obtained by brief sessions of practice spaced over periods of time than by one long session, also that variety in practice facilitates recall and makes training more palatable. This requires hard work and ingenuity on the part of the teacher, but pays off handsomely. One of the pitfalls awaiting the novice teacher of slow learners is her desire to cater to the neurotic restlessness of her charges. She keeps them continually entertained by films and demonstrations in hope that some of it will wear off. In truth, some of it does wear off, but, alas, it does not restore the lost skills needed to find success and self-respect on their own. Fortunately, teaching machines are coming to her rescue. Drill tapes are available on most mathematical processes. Spelling and vocabulary programs can be obtained, and some machines push the reader to a faster pace almost without his being aware. Math, reading, and science laboratories may soon take over the task of supplying a variety of concentrated practice, but the duty of providing solid, basic skills will still remain with the teacher. Don't be misled by the slow learner's indifference. He knows when he is being fed baby food instead of the solid fare he needs, and he will not thank you for it. It is not the three R's he resents, it is the pace, the lack of meaning, the unfair comparisons that alienate him.

The seventh principle—slow learner's instruction must be initiated by careful priming and then painstakingly shaped by increasingly accurate corrections which are reinforced—is a mouthful, (with due credit and apologies to Dr. Skinner) that every parent or pet owner knows. When Fido is to be taught to sit up and beg, his paws are lifted to set him back on his haunches, and if he holds this position for a few seconds, he is rewarded with a biscuit. It works best, of course, if he is a bit hungry. After this is repeated several times, Fido gets the point, and when the command sit-up is given, lifts his paws. But no pet owner is satisfied until the performance is polished, so the act is repeated with corrections, each of which is slightly improved; and if the reward is withheld until each correction is performed properly, Fido soon becomes an old trouper. This is shaping.

It would pay any teacher of slow learners to study Dr. Skinner's technique, since it is ideally suited to their needs. Teachers are usually good at priming behavior, but there they stop. Being unable to reinforce individually each student's response to the prime, that response is soon extinguished. Shaping does take place in most classes, but that too is not reinforced and falls on deaf ears. Thus the learning process is aborted. Fortunately, teaching machines and programmed instruction can now arrange contingencies of reinforcement for the individual student far beyond anything the teacher could accomplish. According to Dr. Skinner: "Two pigeons have been trained (by shaping) to coordinate behavior with a precision which equals the most skillful human dancers."[6] Although humans are not birds and do have minds of their own, with due allowance for this fact, the same techniques are highly adaptable to the classroom and have proven efficacious.

In a school system without machines let us see how this would work using Miss Smith, the tenth grade English teacher. She is teaching the simple sentence and decides to use the prime and shape technique.

Miss Smith, standing before the desk of a front row student, picked up the girl's text book. "Class," she said, "tell me what I just did."

"You stole Susan's book."

Miss Smith, now an old pro, did not bat an eye. "All right," she said, walking to the black board, "write down this sentence. I stole Susan's book. It is a simple sentence."

She copied the sentence large on the black board, exaggerating the capital *I*, the capital *S* of Susan's name, the apostrophe and *s* after "Susan," and the period following the sentence. *This is the prime.*

Now, she went down the aisle. To those who had copied the sentence correctly, she commented, "Good." For others she made the necessary corrections without comment.

[6] Skinner, B.F. *The Technology of Teaching* p 12.

"Now class, write the sentence omitting the subject."

Once again, she made the rounds of the class, complimenting those who were correct—helping those who were wrong. Painstakingly, she shaped their responses to: "Write the sentence without the punctuation showing it to be the beginning of the sentence; write the sentence without the punctuation showing that the book belongs to Susan," etc.

After each task, she complimented and corrected. It is time consuming but thorough and necessary, considering that many slow learners reach high school without being able to write a simple sentence after six years of teaching. While she takes time to check each individual, the remainder of the class is unoccupied and apt to become noisy. This is why machines and teacher's aides will eventually take over such routine and free Miss Smith for more important tasks.

HOW TO MAKE THEM WANT TO LEARN

This question has partly been answered in preceding pages. A student who has been given meaningful material which he can do and then rewarded for his efforts, will, under most circumstances, continue those efforts. *All* slow learners need to be shown that they are able to succeed, and, if circumstances are provided to continue their success, will attempt to do so. This assumes that they have been reached at an early age before their defenses are impenetrable.

The hard core slow learner in middle and high school is a more difficult problem. His hostility to school has so hardened that he will be suspicious and scornful of even the most sincere efforts to help him. Some inducement, meaningful enough to overcome this resentment, must be resorted to. This entails some form of extrinsic reward. The following suggestions have been or could be successfully employed:

1. Work-study programs have been very effective. Earning money is meaningful to slow learners. It renews their self-confidence and self-respect. It enables them to make a fresh start and compete on an equal basis with others. Contact with the realities of the world increases their respect for education, and being able to earn school credits while on the job makes sense to them. If holding a job is contingent on successful classroom participation, it becomes a powerful deterrent to misbehavior and poor attendance.

2. A schedule of positive reinforcements such as candy, tokens, drinks, etc. (if your school system permits) is not difficult to work out and has been used successfully in a number of situations. During a summer institute, in which the author took part, a free coke break contingent upon successful completion of classroom assignment proved effective.

3. During the time in which the author directed a program for potential dropouts, these difficult boys were organized into a club called "Mech-techs" with elected officers. Shop smocks were purchased for each individual with the name "Mech-tech" on the back and the individual's name embroidered over the front pocket. When engaged in projects around the school, such as minor repairs, they were allowed to wear these smocks. They soon became prized possessions. An extension of this idea was proposed but never implemented, although the author feels it would be highly effective with hard core dropouts. The proposal was to install a club room within the school, complete with drink and food dispensing machines as well as pin ball machines. Smoking would also be permitted with parent permission. Membership was to be limited to "Mech-techs" only with limited guest privileges. Rules would be formulated and policed by members themselves, subject to final approval of the principal. Use of the club room could be curtailed for periods of time for infraction of rules, misconduct in class, and lack of classroom progress due to excessive absenteeism. This may sound like a far cry from education, but today's crisis demands new and inventive solutions.

4. Shop programs can be made more meaningful by teaching slow learners to repair their own cars and motorcycles, or to learn odd jobs such as repairs to small appliances. Many of the "Mech-techs" earned money after school by servicing their neighbor's lawn mowers.

HOW TO PRESERVE SELF-RESPECT AND
BUILD EGO STRENGTH

Since the principal ailment of slow learners is self-devaluation due to school failure, it is up to the school to reverse this process and rebuild their self-respect. This can best be done by increasing their school status, demonstrating to them that they can succeed and providing them with tangible evidence of their success in the form of grades.

Dr. James C. Coleman, noted psychologist, states, "Self-approval is hard to achieve or maintain without the confirmation of social approval of the people most important to us."[7] No one, not even a parent, is more important to students than their peers. In most schools, slow learners find themselves at the bottom of the social hierarchy. It is common for the slow classes and work-study students to receive the oldest books, the least desirable classrooms, the ancient furniture. They are seldom elected to student offices or see their names on honor rolls or award lists. They are often left out of school assemblies and sometimes even the yearbook. Small wonder they fail to identify with the school. They harbor a bitterness about this that would surprise some principals. Counselors discover their pathetic craving for social status when attempting realistically to schedule slow learners for vocational or business subjects. Many slow learners refuse these subjects stubbornly, because they bear a low caste rank, not only among students, but among parents. Schools might profitably employ an advertising agency to enhance the prestige of commercial, skilled, and technical curricula. It could drastically reduce the tremendous attrition rate in colleges and provide the nation with skilled technicians. Great numbers of students who enter college

---

[7] Coleman, James C. *Abnormal Psychology and Modern Life.* p 73.

only to drop out after a few semesters could have succeeded in a junior college, technical, or business course.

A concerted effort should be made by schools to provide slow learners with the latest books, colorfully decorated classrooms, modern furniture, and above all, the best teachers. Halls should be decorated with large photos of work-study students or recent graduates on the job. The school newspaper should interview students on the job and publicize their achievements. Slow classes and work-study students need their own clubs that could hold dances, assemblies, and exhibitions. They should have teams of different sports that would engage in inter and intra school contests. These are not impractical ideas. The DECA Clubs of the Distributive Education Courses which receive federal support under the George Barden Act of 1946 and the VICA Clubs of the Industrial Cooperative Training Classes do an outstanding job of helping work-study pupils identify with their schools. But this is only a drop in the bucket compared to what a sympathetic principal could accomplish.

Dr. James C. Coleman states: "One of the important assumptions of an individual's frame of reference is his assumption of the possibility for change, for personal growth and social progress."[8] One of the most baffling aspects of a counselor's work with slow learners is his inability to convince them they can succeed in school by making a few essential, but comparatively easy, changes in their habits. They will simply not accept this possibility unless provided with tangible evidence. Sometimes this evidence must be contrived. The author once had an arrangement with a teacher whereby failing English students, who could not learn vocabulary lists, were referred to him as their counselor. The counselor would go over the list of words with the student, showing him good learning habits. The teacher would then give the

---

[8] Coleman, James C. *Abnormal Psychology and Modern Life* p 63.

student a retest, similar to the original one but much easier. To the student's amazement, he usually made a good grade (the teacher saw to that). The student would return to the counselor the following day with more confidence. This was repeated for several weeks except that each time the teacher made the test a trifle harder. Eventually, the student was making good grades on regular tests, almost without realizing it.

Students rate themselves by grades. It is an erroneous concept, considering how subjective grades are, but still a fact. If the slow learner's self respect is to be restored, schools must find a way for him to compete on an equal basis with more academically-talented youngsters. A society that calls itself democratic can scarcely do less.

PROVIDING OUTLETS FOR THEIR HOSTILITY

One of the principal complaints slow learners have about schools is that little communication occurs between them and the academic, socially-successful students. Second to this is the charge that no understanding exists between them and the faculty. In truth, there is some justification for these charges.

One of the reasons many adopt long hair and bizarre dress is to protest this denial of their identity. Being deprived of the recognition accorded successful students, they turn to anti-establishment behavior as a means of self-fulfillment. Counselors can provide an outlet for their frustrations by sympathetic listening. It is best done in small groups within the school milieu. The term "group therapy" should be strictly avoided. It conveys the connotation of mental illness both to them and to their parents and can only add to their insecurity. Group discussion or group counseling are better terms. Counselors in middle school and high school should be trained in this technique. Allowing dissident students to ventilate their hostility serves to drain off some of it. If care is taken in the selection of group membership so as to include some better-adjusted students who are nevertheless sympathetic with dissenters, beneficial exchange can take place. Protesters will listen to common sense coming from other students which they would summarily reject from adults. A counselor who attempts this must himself be personally secure since the atmosphere of the discussion must be "no holds barred."

A second useful device is a joint student-faculty committee, organized for the express purpose of hearing and investigating complaints. When students know that this resort is available to them, and that their grievances will be heard and treated equitably, much of their antagonism disappears.

DEALING WITH THE DISORGANIZED HOME ENVIRONMENT

Since emotional illness is contracted in the home, it must be treated in the home. Even the best school situation makes little headway if the child must be returned each night to the turmoil that first warped his spirit. It is foolhardy to hope that a counselor or teacher can reverse years of neglect and abuse. Parents of emotionally-disturbed children are often themselves ill and usually resent interference. Children, too, become embarrassed and humiliated at having counselors discover the true conditions under which they live. Before intruding on the privacy of the home, the counselor should always obtain permission. Yet, if genuine concern is shown, home visits can generate enormous good will. No matter how weak or calloused, most parents have affection for their children, and, if approached sincerely, are willing to cooperate. They usually do not understand how their actions affect the child until it is explained to them. A trained counselor can usually detect the cause of stress, particularly if the child has talked freely in a sympathetic relationship. Most families will accept an offer of help if made honestly. Whenever mental health clinics and family welfare agencies are available, the counselor should always refer cases to them with the family's permission, but in the absence or unaccessability of specialized services, the school can still make a beneficial contribution.

DEALING WITH THE HOSTILE COMMUNITY ENVIRONMENT

This will be dealt with at greater length in Chapter 4. It is beyond anything a teacher or counselor can do alone. To be surrounded by a hostile community is disastrous to the learning atmosphere of the school and a tragedy for the students. Since it is practically impossible to separate an individual's values from those of his primary group, the important people in a child's life determine his outlook. If his parents and neighbors downgrade study, nothing teachers say will have any influence on him. Slow learners are most susceptible to this pressure.

The community must be won over by a genuine demonstration of concern for children on the part of school personnel. Contrary to some opinion, inner-city residents put a high value on education. They simply are not convinced that schools are providing the proper kind of learning for their children. The fact that the proportion of dropouts in the inner-city schools is much higher than elsewhere lends credence to their suspicions.

TEACHING THEM NEW RESPONSES TO THE SCHOOL SITUATION

Types of behavior on the part of slow learners which schools term objectionable are learned responses. They have been shaped by the contingencies of the classroom experience. Hostility, withdrawal, attention-seeking are all responses which have been substituted for study, recitation, and research, because the latter responses have gone unrewarded. When first learned, inappropriate responses could have been easily extinguished by not being reinforced and different responses substituted by positive reinforcement; but as the slow learner's defenses take shape, these defenses begin to acquire a reinforcement of their own. If rebellious, slow learners receive satisfaction from demonstrating their independence and courage. If they play the clown, they enjoy the attention that their behavior attracts— at least people know they are there. If withdrawn or negative, they are being nonconformists, and humans have derived pleasure from this since Biblical times. As a student once told the author, "I get a charge out of not doing what people want me to do."

It is true that schools do practice negative reinforcement in the form of reproof and failure, but this only teaches students what to avoid. It does not shape desirable behavior. In most school situations, punishment could not be completely discarded for fear of chaos, but there is a marked tendency on the part of many teachers to use punishment as revenge, which only antagonizes dissidents and challenges them to further defiance. If undesirable responses were simply ignored, they could more easily be extinguished. But extinguishing undesirable responses is not enough. New, more adaptive responses must be initiated and then reinforced. Waiting for such contingencies to take place is time-wasting. A basic rule of operant conditioning is that behavior must take place before it can be reinforced, so the appropriate setting for desirable behavior must be contrived by the teacher.

For example—let us take another look at Gertrude Smith, the tenth grade English teacher of the introduction to this book. She could not be suffering from iron poor blood, having asked for such a difficult assignment in the first place, so let us assume that she went home that night, had a good cry, washed out a few things, and began to prepare tomorrow's lesson plan. She knew that she must initiate new behavior on the part of her non-readers. A glance at the evening paper supplied her with the answer. She slipped out to the drug store and purchased twenty-two newspapers. The next morning, she hid them in her desk until she had taken roll, then made her gambit.

"I see by the newspaper that marijuana is psychologically addictive and should be banned by law."

No sharper goad could have provoked a swifter re-;ponse. The air was filled with cries of outraged rebuttal.

"That ain't so!"

"It don't hurt 'cha!"

"It ain't no worse than alcohol."

At this point, Miss Smith hauled out the newspapers and said, "Show me where it says that in this article."

Whereupon, she handed a newspaper to each student. Not realizing they had been hooked, all began poring over the paper, some using their fingers to trace the lines. Soon a few found passages which they read laborously aloud to support their viewpoints, but they also found some contradictory statements. A lively discussion ensued which lasted all period. Miss Smith wisely did not take up the papers, and she noticed a few turning pages to other sections.

That afternoon she spent several hours after school in the library and came to class the following morning with six books.

"Since you are all so interested in drugs," she announced to the class, "you should know more about them. For instance, you think you have something new going with 'pot.' Did you know that it has been used for centuries in Asia in another form, called hashish? Now, which of you will volunteer to read about a particular drug and report on it to the class? One of you can take cocaine, another heroin, and some one else barbiturates."

The response from the class this time was less than enthusiastic, but a few hands were raised. She handed out the books and made the assignments.

For several days these reports provoked good class discussions, but Miss Smith knew she could not long stay on the subject of drugs, so she again brought twenty-two papers to class one morning.

This time she began by asking each student how they expected to earn a living. Most admitted they had not given the matter much thought. Miss Smith suggested that this would be a good time to start looking through the help wanted ads to find out what jobs were available and what the requirements were to obtain them.

It soon became evident to the class that most jobs required a high school diploma. Miss Smith suggested that they make a study of jobs by inquiring among neighbors and local businesses about the jobs people they knew held, what each paid and what education or training was needed to hold them. Each day these reports were compared with the ads in the papers. More and more students were reading the papers and new topics suggested themselves, such as the draft, the war and the campus riots.

Buying daily papers was putting a strain on Miss Smith's budget, so she persuaded the principal to buy the papers and have them delivered to the school each morning. The cost was really quite nominal.

By the end of two weeks, Miss Smith had acquired among the students the reputation of being a real "neat" teacher. But still she was not satisfied that the discussions fulfilled all the educational needs her charges required. She began to require each student to write a paragraph supporting his point of view. These she read carefully each night and returned the following day with a grade that reflected the effort put into it starting with "C." She made a careful list of each mistake, but made no marks on the papers. In class she went over each mistake, not identifying the culprit but requiring each student to correct his own paper before his grade could be recorded in her book.

At the end of six weeks, Miss Smith's report cards were handed out. There were no D's or F's except for complete non-participation or excessive absence. Some students were almost incredulous at being able to take home the first B they had ever received. The principal, observing that fewer behavior problems were occuring and that there had been a marked increase in attendance, managed to talk the superintendent's office out of twenty-three subscriptions to the *Reader's Digest* and 100 paperback books (quite a few of which were not on the state's approved list).

Now there is free reading several days a week in Miss Smith's class. She still does not have the best behaved class in the school (some of the books have been used for throwing), but she is the proudest teacher. At the Saturday Soc Hops she is never allowed to sit out a dance.

chapter 3

Initiating the Elementary
School Remedial Program

The study of permanent records of secondary school
underachievers inevitably indicts the elementary school as
the staging area for their failure. In many cases it is possible
to pinpoint the exact grade in which their dislike for school
began. If help had been available at the time, their tragedy
might have been averted. It is most imperative that slow
learners and emotionally disturbed children be quickly identified before irreparable harm to their egos has taken place.
This chapter will deal with the diagnosis and remedial
teaching of those students who begin to falter in the early
grades. Once they have been allowed to build a protective
shield against humiliation, the task becomes almost in-
surmountable.

The slow learner only discovers that he differs from
other children after he enters school. When that happens he
needs a skillful and understanding teacher to soften the
blow. He must first understand that all children differ in a
variety of ways, none of which make them any more or less
desirable as people. Second, he must realize that he has many
important abilities not as yet developed. Last, he must believe

that his present difficulty can be remedied by he and the teacher working together. His teacher must be sincere enough to convince him that he is prized and accepted for himself alone. No child should be failed at this impressionable age. Failure carries with it the stigma of inferiority, and he will wear it like a badge as long as he is in school and occasionally for life.

Unfortunately, even the best-intentioned teachers can convey non-verbal disapproval to the slow learner, and even worse, to other children in the class. When this happens, the other children parrot her attitude with puerile cruelty. If she shows impatience when correcting his mistakes or draws attention to him when making assignments that differ from others, the slow learner becomes alarmed and sensitive to any slight that reveals his inferiority. If changes in his material must be made, they should be done routinely when a variety of activities is taking place. Above all, no comparison should ever be implied as to the relative difficulty of the materials. Over a period of time, it cannot be kept from the slow learner that he is receiving special attention, but if he has had time to internalize this fact and has enjoyed some success with his new material, he will welcome this attention. The following true episode illustrates how easily a school problem can be created.

> Jim, age seven and large for his age, had always been more athletic, more aggressive than other children in his neighborhood. He could climb higher, run faster, and throw a ball further than the rest. This ability had made him something of a bully, but still the envy of his companions; and it was Jim who initiated the games and led a group of smaller, admiring imitators at play.
>
> But today the tables had turned. As a matter-of-fact, Jim had steadily been losing his confidence since the start of this year. Reading was proving difficult, and as previously, Jim was having trouble with the first line of a story the second grade was reading. His voice was barely

audible as he omitted several words and mispronounced others.

"Try again, Jim," Miss Graham encouraged, "it isn't hard. Susan will help you."

He started again, but at the first mistake, a distinct snicker was heard from the rear of the class. Jim glanced apprehensively over his shoulder, but innocent faces were all glued to their books. Susan was crowding his shoulder, now eager to demonstrate her skill. She glibly rattled off the sentence, then looked to the teacher for approval.

"Very good, Susan," Miss Graham complimented, "Jim, I have another book I think you'll find easier. Come up to the desk and we'll read it together. Children, you continue with the story silently."

As Jim followed Miss Graham, something froze inside him. He didn't understand it, but somehow he knew he was no longer leader of his gang. Maybe after school—in the yard—things would be the same again, but in this classroom he was suddenly afraid. He looked out the window and longed desperately to be out in the sunshine. Abruptly, he broke into tears and darted for the door.

The next day he was not in school. The principal called Jim's home and at noon, Jim's father brought him in, tearful and defiant. Thus began a bitter feud between Jim and the school, punctuated with truancies and misbehavior.

PRESCHOOL AND KINDERGARTEN

Cognitive psychologists maintain that one half of a child's mature intelligence is formed by the age of four, and that his life style is fixed by the age of five. If this is true, schools need to reach children while characteristics so vital to their adult lives can still be shaped. Kindergartens and preschools are one answer to this problem. Private institutions such as the Montesorri schools have for some time been available to the well-to-do, but much more desperate is the need of the disadvantaged child who is starved for the varieties of stimulation provided in middle class homes. "Project Head Start" for preschool children, financed by federal funds under the Elementary and Secondary School Act, has been widely praised by educators as a welcome solution to this problem.

Such programs are a boon to the slow learner, because he can succeed as well as other children without special help. Success in preschool will give him confidence and security that may sustain him when he later encounters difficulties using higher symbols and abstractions. Some teachers insist they can identify slow learners in preschool, but this is highly doubtful. At any rate it should be avoided at all costs since it is unnecessary and may cause great harm.

Some successful methods used with preschool children are as follows:

1. *Discovery*—Fitting blocks and sticks together to construct objects. Using a balance to weigh different size containers of liquids and solids both filled and empty.

2. *Manipulation and Visual Perception*—Taking blocks and spheres apart and assembling them again. Fitting different-sized sticks into proper slots. Teaching discrimination of sizes, colors, shapes, rotation, left to right and top to bottom orientation with colored three-dimensional blocks and tiles.

3. *Curiosity*—Exploring numbers and space with games, puzzles, clocks, and spinners; also counting with brightly-colored counters and an abacus.

4. *Learning Readiness and Sensory Motor Discrimination*—Teaching classification, labeling, drawing conclusions, and recognizing and associating names with objects through the use of colored transparencies on an overhead projector.

5. *Self-Expression*—Painting, drawing, listening to music, and dancing.

6. *Sensory Learning*—Assembling words and numbers with brightly-colored, plastic letters and those cut from sandpaper whose shape can be traced with the fingers.

7. *Social Skills, Attitudes and Personal Habits*—This may be the most important learning of all for children from disorganized homes and neighborhoods, where emotional development now takes place prior to entrance into school.

Materials for the foregoing activities are obtainable from various companies[1], or can be inexpensively constructed in home and school work shops. Their variety has no limit but the ingenuity of the teacher.

Emphasis in teaching is placed on individual instruction, and the teaching ratio kept to one to four or five. This allows much needed interaction between adult and child. The class room should be loosely structured, and, within reason, children should be allowed to do whatever interests them. Since their attention span is short, new stimulation must constantly be introduced.

As yet, no studies are available to estimate the effect preschool will have on a child's later life, but it appears to hold great promise for the disadvantaged child whose attitude toward school and society is more a product of his social position than of his intelligence. All humans tend to adopt a role in society which to them feels comfortable. This role is usually dictated by their primary group, the family, and community. If this group is lower class, their language remains limited and colloquial. Their distrust of agencies of government such as schools and health services prevents them from taking advantage of opportunities offered by society, but even more restricting is their stunted belief in possibilities for self-improvement. These characteristics do not represent intelligent thinking but are acquired customs and habits. Social scientists tell us it is impossible to separate an individual's attitude from that of the group with which he identifies. Yet, if slum children are to profit by education and by learning skills necessary to hold satisfactory jobs, many of their attitudes must be changed.

In a recent research project sponsored by the Research

---

[1] J.H. Pence Company, 119 East Church Ave., Box 863, Roanoke, Virginia.
Science Research Associates, Inc. 259 East Erie St., Chicago, Illinois.
Noble and Noble Publishers, Inc. 750 Third Ave., New York, N.Y. 10017.
Harper and Row, Publishers, Inc., 250 Crawford Ave., Evanston, Illinois.
Western Publishing Co., Inc. Educational Division. School and Library Department. 150 Parish Dr., Wayne, N.J.

Division of the Department of the Children's Bureau, Social Security administration,[2] Virginia C. Shipman and Robert D. Hess hypothesized that "Behavior Which Leads to Social, Educational and Economic Poverty is Socialized in Early Childhood—That it is Learned." Their project "Focused upon the role of the mother as a socializing agency in areas of behavior usually associated with success in school: language, concept development, motivation for achievement, problem-solving strategy, curiosity, and the like." When given tests designed to measure strengths in these areas, it was found that middle-class mothers and their children both scored consistently higher than lower-class mothers and their children. This led Shipman and Hess to conclude, "The lower-class mother's narrow range of alternates is being conveyed to the children through language styles which convey her attitude of fewer options and little individual power, and this is reflected in the child's cognitive development."

In the future, preschools can reach a child before his social position is frozen and can introduce him to a different learning environment which does not restrict his ability to grow. In later life he may develop a substitute set of habits, concepts, and values which will exist side by side with those of his primary group and allow him the option of free choice of the culture with which to identify.

IDENTIFYING THE GENUINE SLOW LEARNER

By the term "genuine slow learner" is meant the child whose academic abilities do not permit him to advance as far

---

[2]Shipman, Virginia C. and Hess, Robert D. "Conceptual Development in Preschool Children: Effects of Home and Family." *The New Elementary School.* Association for Supervision and Curriculum Development. NEA. Washington, D.C.

and as fast as the average student. Using the Stanford-Binet Intelligence Scale Manual, they comprise about 14.5% of the Standardization Group and score between 80 and 89. Those scoring below 80 are not truly educable in the normal school situation and require special education. They can be trained to become happy and useful citizens, but this requires special skills taught at a number of universities and will not be dealt with in this book. If the genuine slow learner's academic situation is not complicated by emotional problems or cultural deprivation, he usually is a happy, social child who will cheerfully and doggedly work at school assignments. He often possesses special talents such as musical, artistic, athletic, or mechanical abilities which compensate for his academic handicap and afford him the success and recognition he needs. Pretty girls are peculiarly able to surmount academic deficiencies. If given material at which he can enjoy success instead of failure, he can progress through school to graduation; and with sufficient motivation, even complete business, trade, or technical school, after which he disappears into society and loses his label.

By suitable material is meant:

1. He can learn to read newspapers, magainzes, and paperback books which appeal to his interests, but he will not understand classical literature.
2. He can learn addition, subtraction, multiplication, division, fractions, decimals, percentage, and simple geometry, but he will never master the commutative, associative, and distributive principles or algebraic formulas.
3. He can write a paragraph and a simple paper, but will never conquer grammar nor write themes and research papers requiring organization.
4. He may take an additional year to reach a satisfactory level in elementary school but will probably not reach sixth grade level by that time—which, of course, is a meaningless term.

Genuine slow learners can be identified as early as the

first grade by their scores on achievement tests. These scores usually fall in the lower quartile. Some tests suitable for this purpose are:

Stanford Achievement Tests[3]
Metropolitan Reading Readiness Test.
SRA Achievement Series.[4]
California Achievement Tests.[5]

Achievement tests are not positive identification, since many above-average children with emotional problems or cultural deprivation also score low. A more reliable fix can be obtained from their scores on individual intelligence tests which fall below 90. Group intelligence tests in elementary school are extremely unreliable. Whenever possible, an individual test such as the Stanford-Binet Intelligence Scale or the Weschler Intelligence Scale for Children should be administered by a trained professional.

This seems to be an appropriate place to discuss intelligence tests. They are undoubtedly culture bound and unfair to the deprived child. Moreover, they do not measure many kinds of intelligence as shown by their low correlation with success in life. However, they do forecast quite accurately success in the normal school situation when properly administered. At best, they are only guides, and if a child masters material assigned to him more rapidly than anticipated, a reevaluation is obviously called for. Arguments against them are generally academic. A child must start at his current functioning level and proceed from there. The starting level can only be the one at which his achievement tests show him to be. If this is too low he will soon demonstrate that fact. No student should ever be frozen into a track or group. If achievement tests as described are not available,

---

[3] Harcourt, Brace and World, Inc. 757 Third Ave. New York, N.Y.
[4] Science Research Associates, Inc. 259 East Erie St. Chicago, Ill.
[5] California Test Bureau. Del Monte Research Park. Monterey California.

it is not difficult for teachers to devise their own diagnostic instruments, so long as they realize that these tests are merely rough guides.

Slow learners should never be graded in competition with average or above average students, nor should they ever be failed in elementary schools. They should be praised and rewarded for progress no matter how small. Parents should be kept informed by meaningful oral or written reports without assigning letter or number grades. If such grades are demanded, the child should be graded on his own progress from his starting point. If he deserves an A for this, he should get it.

To summarize, genuine slow learners present no real problem to any school willing to face up to their needs.

IDENTIFYING THE EMOTIONALLY DISTURBED CHILD

This is vastly more baffling than identifying the genuine slow learner. Emotionally disturbed children are more numerous, they have a bewildering array of problems and no useful tests to ferret them out exist. Yet, the emergency of their situation in our schools continues to grow. To illustrate, in a recent survey of the first grade in a well-run elementary school in Fairfax County, Virginia, 66% were found "likely to experience difficulty and require special programs to meet their needs." This was not in the inner-city but in a relatively affluent suburb of Washington, D.C. with a mixture of middle and lower class and a sprinkling of culturally deprived children. The culturally deprived child may or may not be emotionally disturbed, but he suffers from a similar malady. He has a distortion of reality that weakens his desire and ability to learn. Some genuine slow learners were included in the 66%; therefore, we are faced with three distinct types of children who have special needs to be met.

1. The genuine slow learner.
2. The average or above average child whose emotional problems interfere with his learning.
3. The culturally deprived.
4. Any combinations of the above.

The first screening must of necessity be physical. A child with a handicap such as impaired sight, hearing, or speech needs more help than a classroom teacher can give. Some children come to school with diseases that attenuate their ability to learn and some from disorganized homes are simply tired or hungry most of the time, both of which are destructive to concentration. All schools need specialized services to aid handicapped children such as doctors, dentists, ophthalmologists, hearing and speech therapists, and welfare agencies. A very few children may exhibit bizarre symptoms such as hyperactivity, mutism, extreme withdrawal or fright, rigidity, or other irrational behavior requiring the services of a psychiatrist. Such children need special schools or institutional care beyond that of the public school which is not designed to properly treat them.

This leaves us with a substantial number of children who are apparently normal yet not operating up to their capacity. These are the emotionally disturbed. Testing these children is frustrating. No test can validly be given to a disinterested or uncooperative child. Various personality tests to diagnose emotional ills exist, but the results have little meaning to teachers and are a source of disagreement even among psychologists. Most emotionally disturbed children score low on achievement tests, although a few score high but still produce nothing in school. Regardless of their unreliability, achievement tests are the only instruments suitable for placement. A child can only be started on the level at which he functions, and at which he can enjoy success. If this level proves to be erroneous, a reevaluation is in order.

The only serviceable diagnosis of emotional disturbance

is by teacher observation. All children, at times, exhibit symptoms of emotional illness, but the true problem child will display a pattern identifiable by its persistence and intensity. The following traits may exist alone or in various constellations: belligerence, fighting, truancy, attention-seeking, bullying, and rebellion. Other children may be shy, withdrawn, sullen, or negative. A third type, and uncontestably the most baffling, is the passive-aggressive, who is outwardly friendly and cooperative, but who works hard at producing nothing, offering countless excuses for his failure. Some traits neurotic children have in common are: short attention spans, untidy appearance or bizarre dress, absentmindedness resulting in lost books, pencils, and instructional materials, lack of energy for consistent effort, and, at the same time sustaining vigorous random activity. They seem in a constant tug-of-war with the school to frustrate all efforts to educate them.

DEVELOPING THE REMEDIAL PROGRAM

Upon entrance to school and at least yearly, or whenever necessary thereafter, all children with special needs should be given achievement tests to determine their level of functioning in various areas, the most important of these being reading and mathematics.

When the proper level has been determined, the child should be started there and allowed to progress at his own pace. The nongraded elementary school is so ideal for this purpose that it is difficult to understand why it has not been universally adopted, since any individual may operate at several so-called grade levels at the same time. For example, he may do mathematics at the third grade level, music at the fifth grade level but read only at the second grade. He may be able to master so-called third grade mathematics in six months yet take two years to learn to read at the third grade level. Add to this the facts that girls mature from one to two years ahead of boys and that maturity in any child can vary as much as four years from his chronological age and the concept of grade level becomes an absurdity. Pity the poor teacher trying to adjust instruction to thirty children spanning as much as four grade levels. The nongraded elementary school makes it possible to assign a slow learner to a basic room according to his age, yet take reading, math, science, and social studies elsewhere at his functioning level. He may take more than a year to achieve a satisfactory level in any subject without failing. This is the crucial point. *He must not fail.* He must be graded on his own progress, not in competition with others. He must have the same chance for success and recognition for his achievement as any child no matter how this achievement compares with their's.

Since most systems do not as yet have nongraded elementary schools, an approximation of the same program can be achieved by any enterprising principal with six grades. For the primary grades, one through three, a nongraded Language Development Center and a nongraded Mathematics Laboratory can be set up to which students can be assigned out of their basic rooms for two or more hours per day. A similar arrangement can be made for grades four through six. It is possible for a slow learner to attend his basic class for only two hours a day and spend the balance at various graded and nongraded levels. He can then be retained in reading and mathematics as long as necessary without being retained in his basic grade level class. A typical fourth grade student's schedule might be as follows:

Basic room—fourth grade
Reading Development Center—nongraded
Math Laboratory—nongraded
Social studies—third grade
Science—third grade

At the end of the year he can be advanced as follows:

Basic room—fifth grade
Reading Development Center—nongraded
Math Laboratory—nongraded
Social Studies—fourth grade
Science—fourth grade

The objection the traditional educator has to this is that the student never reaches sixth grade. The reply, of course, is: "What is sixth grade level?" It is the level which the average student reaches by age eleven. But we are not dealing with mythical average students; we are dealing with discrete individuals. The slow learner only advances from one half to three quarters of a grade per year. He can only be expected to achieve the maximum level he is capable of by age eleven. If he has been treated with respect and understanding and has had the opportunity to succeed at his own level of ability, he will reach his maximum and look forward to continuing school.

ORGANIZING THE REMEDIAL TEAMS

Abolishing or adjusting grade levels so that all students can be assigned lessons suitable to their ability or functioning level may be all that is needed for genuine slow learners— alas, for emotionally disturbed children it is not sufficient. A child with a well-developed defense system lacks the will to help himself. He needs somebody to work with him, someone he trusts and with whom he can identify. He needs to be reassured, guided and prompted. A self-starter he is not, and worst of all, he is a nonfinisher. In most cases, his self-image is that of failure, and left to his own initiative, he will soon find ways to prove that his self-image is true. He is a living example of the self-fulfilling prophecy. Moreover, no matter how understanding the school may be, if his home problem is unsolvable he will make little progress. Either his home problem must be corrected or he must be taught to live with it and complete his education in spite of it.

Every elementary school should be staffed with a number of remedial teams to take over a child when he begins to fall behind. These teams would consist of a social worker or counselor, an English instructor, and a math instructor. One counselor per school could work with several remedial teams. She should visit the homes of the children needing help to determine the nature of the home situation and to work, if possible, with parents. She should be the one to formulate the plan for the remedial team and for other of the child's teachers to follow and to coordinate their actions as long as necessary. There should be a number of English and math instructors, so that each can work with individual children or with small groups of three or four. These instructors do not need a bachelor's degree. Teacher's aides are quite satisfactory, and in many cases, even superior to college-trained personnel, since they often feel more empathy for a handicapped child's needs. Four to six aides working in the Language Development Center and the Mathematics Laboratory can handle the requirements of an elementary school with a population of three hundred. If funds are not available for teacher's aides, high school seniors in need of funds for college may be employed. In Fairfax County Virginia schools a number of high school students are working in the elementary schools as part of the high school's Industrial Cooperative Program, whereby they go to school half a day and work for half a day. Older grade school children have also been used successfully in a number of elementary schools in various parts of the United States. A return to the cooperative spirit of the "little red school house" might be a welcome relief from the competitiveness of our impersonal class rooms.

PROVIDING COUNSELING SERVICES

Few elementary schools are staffed, at present, with counselors, but it is a neglect that must be repaired. While it is true that the majority of successful elementary school pupils make progress in spite of this lack, the fact that 66% of a first grade is found in need of specific aid is a powerful argument for counseling services. If slow learners are to be given adequate attention, some type of counseling is a must.

Elementary school counseling is probably a job for a woman, since small children are less likely to give their confidence to a man. In addition, she should have some education or training in social work. Unless a visiting teacher is also available, the counselor will find herself spending much of her time in the community. There are four major areas where her services will prove of significant importance:

1. *Testing*—The most essential knowledge for teaching slow learners is to know their approximate capabilities and at what level they are functioning. Unless the subject matter is appropriate to their needs, all else planned for them will fail. At present, elementary school testing is highly unreliable. A glance at a few permanent records will confirm this fact. While tests from the eighth through the twelfth grade show a fairly consistent pattern, scores for the elementary grades fluctuate widely. Some of this may be attributed to immaturity, yet scores on successive individually-administered tests in elementary school are remarkably stable. Much of the difficulty is due to the use of untrained and often unsympathetic personnel. The counselor will need to instruct teachers and supervise testing closely. In fact, the need is so great that she must beware that too much of her time is not dissapated in this one dimension.

2. *Family Service*—Very few emotional problems originate with the school although the school can aggravate them. It is the emotionally-laden interpersonal relationship of the family that creates problems. The counselor needs to be well-acquainted with the child's home conditions if she is to accurately diagnose and

recommend a course of action to be followed by teachers and principal. Many disorganized homes are in desperate need of a host of services which the knowledgeable counselor can summon from community agencies. Some of these she can supply herself. Once again, she must be cautious not to squander too much of her time at this task. A weak family will latch onto someone with ego strength for support with a dispairing grip. The counselor must remember that only the child is her responsibility and that she may be his last and only hope.

3. *Providing Insight About Pupils*—The counselor alone may know the child as an individual. Teachers tend to evaluate a child in terms of his progress or to see his performance only as a member of a group. His defenses often obscure the real child cowering behind them, and the role he plays to hide his feelings of inferiority from both teachers and peers is a distorted caricature of his true self. Only in the security of a non-judgemental one-to-one relationship will his real identity become apparent. Parents, teachers and principal all have a stake in his progress. What he needs is a friend who is interested in him only as a person. It cannot be emphasized too strongly that this will not be accomplished simply by listening. The counselor must visit him in the class room, on the play ground, and outside of school. She must be prepared to intervene for him with authorities, if necessary, to prove to him that she is a true friend and deserving of his confidence.

4. *Providing Support to Handicapped Students*—Every pupil needs the security of adult support but none so much as the failing student who cannot find it in his own home. He truly "does not have a friend in the world." Disorganized families are only one example. Many parents are simply too busy or too involved with other problems to cope with the child's inability to master school. Not knowing what to do, they throw the problem back onto the school. The teacher and principal, having their hands full with many other children, in turn pass the responsibility on to the counselor. It is too much to expect that she can shoulder this burden alone, but with her the buck stops. She must do what she can to be his confidant, to reassure his doubts, to restore his confidence, and to help him set new goals. She may even have to teach him to insulate his feelings, to detach himself emotionally from his home environment, and to learn to depend on himself alone. To tell the truth, she is not often successful. It is a time-consuming job about which little is yet known.

DEALING WITH THE DISRUPTIVE CHILD

The New York City school teachers' strike drew considerable attention to the problem of the disruptive child. It cannot be denied that this type of student is an obstacle to a successful class room. Little learning takes place in a disorganized and undisciplined atmosphere, and no teacher should be expected to engage in a contest for control of her class while she is concentrating on the needs of thirty pupils willing to learn. Moreover, it is undemocratic to sacrifice the welfare of the many to the discontent of the few. The disruptive child represents an antisocial force, destructive to the best interests of our society.

Where measures to meet the needs of each individual in the elementary school, as previously outlined in this chapter, are instituted, the numbers of disruptive children should diminish to a manageable size. Yet this child's problems are many, and it is too much to expect that he will soon disappear from our schools. Expelling him is no solution, since this merely transfers the problem to areas even more dangerous to society. Moreover, disruptive children also have a right to education which the school must recognize.

The disruptive child is not solely to blame for his attitude. School and society must share the guilt. He may be the product of two deadly psychological forces, a poor home environment and an educational climate unresponsive to his needs. At home his discipline has been one of two types: he may have been inconsistently punished at the whim of tyrannical adults who have made no attempt to teach him why he was wrong or to reward him when he was right, or even worse, he may have been raised by adults who were too weak or too disinterested to discipline him at all. In either case he has grown up with no respect for authority. His only learned response to discipline is hostility.

At school he has met nothing but frustration. Lacking the self-discipline to study, he does not learn and soon suffers the humiliation of failure. He is the object of scorn by teachers, administrators, and fellow students. Receiving no reward or reinforcement for his efforts, he soon comes to hate school and the society which forces him to endure this captive degradation.

Everyone, adult or child, must have "something going for them," if for no other reason than to prove that they are people and not ciphers. The only thing the disruptive child has "going for him" is the recognition he receives for his misbehavior and defiance. Other children, better trained or more fearful, receive a vicarious thrill from the disruptive child's challenge to authority and accord him the notoriety upon which his ego feeds.

The first step in dealing with the disruptive child is to deny him his reward. He must be removed from his admiring audience quietly and firmly, but without hostility. If he is treated with patience and compassion but with no sign of weakness, he will receive little reinforcement for his bravado.

The second step must be a process of reconditioning. Since he knows only one way to react to authority, he must be taught a new and better way. Two or three such students can be taken over by a teacher's aide in a secluded spot where the process of education can continue without an audience. Nothing will be accomplished for a while, but the habits of school are strong, and eventually he will make halfhearted efforts. Any effort, no matter how small, should be recognized and rewarded. It is possible that material rewards such as soft drinks or candy bars may be necessary at first, since the reinforcement, to be effective, must be immediate and meaningful. Over a period of time, his efforts, finding some reinforcement, will increase and can be shaped. Finding himself learning and recognized for his learning, he will then receive the true reinforcement all children crave. He should be returned to the class room as soon as possible. When disruptive behavior again occurs, the whole process must be repeated. This scheme requires great skill and patience on the part of the school, but there appears no effective alternate than to dump the disruptive child onto society where he soon becomes a vicious and costly menace.

ESTABLISHING A SPECIAL MIDDLE SCHOOL PREPARATORY PROGRAM

Separate classes for academic cripples are usually unsatisfactory, since segregation of any sort carries with it the stigma of inferiority, destructive to a child's ego. Such classes may, however, be inevitable. Transfers may be received from other schools where no attempt has been made to meet their needs, and even in the best schools, children from disorganized families will be found whose ego strength is insufficient to enable them to reach a satisfactory level by the end of the sixth grade. Sending them on to certain disaster in middle school is an even worse solution than special classes. If an additional year of remedial work is needed, they should be retained, but failure should not be added to their ordeal. The school should emphasize to student and parent alike that the child has not failed sixth grade but needs additional time to prepare for middle school. Promotion from this special class should be automatic with the possible exception of nonattendance. Membership should carry as much status as the school can summon. Its members should be treated as the school's senior citizens and given commensurate privileges and positions of trust. Such status symbols could include:

1. A special table in the cafeteria.
2. Assignment as clerical workers in the office and library.
3. Operators of visual aid and audio equipment.

4. Guarding crossings, halls, and playground.
5. Supervision of smaller children in games on the playground.
6. Organization into a club with elected officers for use in community work and charity drives.

The teacher of the Middle School Preparatory Program should be a man, preferably an athlete with whom boys can identify. The class should be housed in a separate room having its own library of magazines, newspapers, and paper back books appealing to teen-agers. Instruction should be devoted almost entirely to English and mathematics, some of which would be taught in a Programmed Instruction Center where students could work alone in carrels. Older students who know they are deficient are extremely sensitive. They often do nothing so as not to demonstrate their weakness to the teacher and classmates alike. If allowed to work alone in the privacy of a carrel they will work much better since no one can observe their mistakes. Teaching machines (where unavailable—tape recordings and view finders can be used) have a number of advantages: they are uncritical, uncondescending, and possess unlimited patience. Moreover, they can concentrate on repairing specific weakness brought to light by diagnostic tests.

A number of companies market suitable machines. The Programmed Instruction Center for Basic Education at Fort Belvior, Virginia, operated by the United States Army uses the Craig Reader[6] which is supplied with lessons ranging from the fourth to the twelfth grade designed to increase vocabulary, word recognition and reading speed. Fort Belvoir also uses the Welch Autotutor Mark III.[7] Programmed

---

[6] Manufactured by Craig Research, Inc. 3410 South La Cienega Blvd. Los Angeles, California.
[7] Manufactured by Welch Scientific Co. Skokie, Illinois.

lessons for this machine are coordinated with California diagnostic Tests.[8] Specific tapes are supplied to correct deficiencies found by testing.

Project CABEL (Center for Adult Basic Educational Learning), located in Northern Virginia, one of 21 experimental and demonstration projects funded by the U.S. Office of Education, uses LEARNING 100, a multi-media communication skills system developed by Educational Development Laboratories, Inc.[9] It has a basic program for the equivalent of first, second and third grade level, and an intermediate program for students reading at fourth through sixth grade level. Film strips are provided with the EDL Controlled Reader and the EDL Tach-X Tachistoscope. Although still in the experimental stage, they seem to hold great promise for teaching language to the slow learner and particularly to the culturally disadvantaged.

After a poor start, industrial giants such as IBM, Xerox and General Learning Corporation are researching and revising soft ware for teaching machines. Education badly needs modern technology to free teachers for more productive work, to relieve hard-pressed tax payers, and to help students learn in new and dynamic ways. What technology can accomplish is delightfully demonstrated by the popular television program *Sesame Street.*

A word of caution is necessary regarding the purchase of expensive hardware. Countless studies have borne out the fact that it is still the teacher who makes the difference. Good teachers will only be produced by better training, better pay, and better recognition. Motivation to learn from any technique including machines will only be generated when schools provide success and reinforcement for all students.

---

[8] California Test Bureau. McGraw Hill Book Company. Del Monte Research Park, Monterey, California.
[9] Educational Development Laboratories. A division of McGraw-Hill. Huntington, New Jersey.

FINDING SUITABLE MATERIALS

Specific techniques for teaching slow learners will be detailed in later chapters, but some new and effective devices now available are as follows:

1. Language Experience in Reading for first and second graders. This is a total language arts approach, encompassing reading, writing, spelling listening and speaking, using children's own experiences and vocabulary. [10]

2. The Listening Master, for use in the school's Language Development Center for grades one through three. The child places in the machine a card on which is reproduced a picture with its name. The child pronounces the word then throws a switch. The machine reproduces his voice aloud to him followed by the correct pronunciation. [11]

3. The Listening Center, useful in the Language Development Center, grades one through three. It has a hook-up for eight ear phones. The child can listen to a recording telling the story in his book while he reads silently. [12]

4. The SRA Reading Laboratory is a series useful in the Language Development Center, grades one through three. It consists of 44 color-coded word building games designed to help students develop a reading vocabulary to match their listening vocabulary. [13]

5. The SRA Reading Laboratory Series grades four through six has skill building materials that span a number of ability levels. [14]

6. The AAAS Science Program produced by the American Association of the Advancement of Science furnishes material for each lesson of an experimental discovery approach for grades one through three. Additional grades will soon be available. [15]

---

[10] Produced by Encyclopaedia Britannica Educational Corp. 425 North Michigan Ave., Chicago, Illinois.

[11] Manufactured by Audio Fidelity Corporation. Richmond, Virginia.

[12] Manufactured by Rheim Califoné. Los Angeles, California.

[13] Produced by Science Research Associates, Inc. 259 East Erie Street, Chicago, Illinois 60611.

[14] *Ibid.*

[15] Distributed by Xerox Corporation. Education Division 1735 I St. N.W. Washington, D.C.

7. Tape recorders are very useful in the Language Development Center to analyze the individual's speech patterns for clarity, communication and pronunciation, and to reinforce listening skills.

8. Viewlex Previewer Jr. permits individual students to scan film strips of social studies while tapes are being played. These tapes are available in multi-level degrees of difficulty. [16]

9. Television sets which can be rolled from room to room keep in touch with educational television stations.

10. Overhead projectors are great teaching aides when used with transparencies. These can easily be made locally, but excellent colored transparencies can be obtained from many companies. [17]

11. Mathematics Laboratory equipment such as mock-ups, manual and visual aids, visuals, programmed instruction materials, and drill tapes are available from many companies. [18]

All of the foregoing materials are now in use in the Fairfax County, Virginia public schools and in various other parts of the country.

---

[16] Available from Viewlex Inc. Holbrook, N.J.

[17] Stanley Bowman Co., Inc. Valhalla, New York. Milligan Publishing Co. St. Louis, Missouri. Creative Visuals 819 Broad St., Richmond, Virginia.

[18] EDL Laboratories. Huntington, New York. Teacher's Publishing Co. Darien, Connecticut.

McGraw-Hill Publishing Co. 330 West 42nd St. New York, N.Y.

Science Research Associates. 259 East Erie St. Chicago, Illinois.

Harcourt Brace & World. Special Projects Department 757 Third Ave., New York, N.Y.

Scott Foresman & Co. Glenville, Illinois

J.H. Pence Co. 119 East Church, Virginia Box 863 Roanoke, Virginia.

chapter 4

Teaching the Disadvantaged Child

It would be presumptious to join the polemic dust-raising that has accompanied attempts to improve the instruction of disadvantaged children after so many prominent educators have taken a turn. To date, it remains a dilemma that has baffled state and federal departments of education, several eminent foundations, and a few esteemed universities. This chapter will attempt only to make some common sense suggestions. At least, common sense never made a situation worse. Some of these suggestions may not be popular, but they are fundamental to a solution, if indeed there is a solution.

1. Heartless as it seems, adults are using children as pawns in an ideological struggle which the children do not understand; a struggle in which they have little to gain but a lifetime to lose. It is high time the welfare of children became the sole criterion for operating schools. Too much adult prestige has already been committed.

2. Disadvantaged children, like all other children, need someone interested in them as individuals. Money, buildings, social theories, or control of schools will not satisfy their need for the security of sympathetic adult relationships.

3. All other considerations are dwarfed by the need to prepare them to become independent, self-respecting members of our working community. A man who has a job and can support his family is usually a respected husband and father. He can usually take care of his other problems.

4. Despite the turbulent pictures of mankind's unruliness, magnified by the communication media, the world is moving toward a better-planned, more integrated society. This trend is being dictated by the inexorable pressures of population growth. But more significant is the picture of the future being unreeled before our eyes. Mankind's most stupendous project, the moon shot, has been accomplished by science, planning, and discipline. The people involved are highly skilled and educated. It predicts more education for everyone. It portends a planned, organized, disciplined society in which racism of any kind will be an anachronism. Literally, from now on, nothing is beyond man's capacity to change or improve.

The term "disadvantaged" will be used interchangably with another synonym, "culturally-deprived." Both describe children from families where the standards of living and culture are below the national minimum. These children are deficient in basic skills, especially in verbal ability. Their knowledge of the world is narrow and vague. The Educational Policies Commission describes the disadvantaged as follows: "They are less able than better educated persons to be trained for skilled positions. They have little of the understanding required of wise consumers. Often they and their children reject schooling. Inferior and overpriced housing further handicaps their health, education, and ability to support themselves. By misuse of property, they further impair their living conditions. Their residential concentration multiplies their problems and retards the learning of new ways. Mistrust of government and civic apathy also hinder their adaptation. Racial discrimination compounds the difficulties of many. Poverty and disease continue to plague them; deliquency and crime rates rise; and the society at large appears remote and uninterested."[1]

There is an even more important obstacle to their education evident to those who work with them. It is the lack of faith in the possibility of change. They seem unable to visualize themselves as escaping the imprisonment of their barren surroundings by upward mobility. Facing the world without the security of their familiar environment and the brotherhood of their friends and neighbors is so threatening that they neglect opportunities to improve their education or seek better employment.

Disadvantaged conditions are customarily thought to apply to the minorities comprising the Negro, Puerto Rican, Spanish-American, and Indian reservation children, but it has been estimated that more than ten times as many whites are similarily handicapped.

There is no one disadvantaged type. Obviously, the timid, fawn-eyed child of the deep South sharecropper who does not even know his first name is a world apart from the aggressive, resourceful gang-member of the ghetto. No one educational program or special project can accommodate such a span. Teachers, counselors, and administrators must fit their programs to their own situations. One requirement, however is paramount—whatever is adopted must suit each individual child.

WHAT DO THEY WANT—WHAT DO THEY NEED?

The obvious reply to both questions is: They need and want the same studies as other children. To suggest that any

---

[1] National Education Association and American Association of School Administrators, Educational Policies Commission. *Education and the Disadvantaged American.* Washington, D.C.: the Commission, 1962. p 5.

group of Americans be taught a non-standard curriculum is insulting. Besides, black, brown and white capitalists alike need to hire employees who speak and behave like average Americans.

Despite some discouraging results from achievement tests, disadvantaged children need pre-school training. The understandings they will acquire cannot be measured by standard tests. Pre-school curriculum should not differ from that taught other children so long as it is tailored to the needs of the individual child. This curriculum has already been described in Chapter 3, but will necessarily change with new discoveries and experience.

Elementary school curriculum should also be as outlined in Chapter 3 with several possible additions:

1. In the predominately disadvantaged schools, standard English should be taught for specific purposes. Where, as in some Mexican-American communities, the children do not understand English at all, school should be taught in Spanish by a bilingual teacher while English is being learned. Speech therapy is almost a prerequisite to successful reading instruction. This does not mean the child's colloquial language needs to be corrected or downgraded. It is so much a part of the child's identity it must be preserved to prevent damage to his self-esteem. Rather, teachers should learn to accept the pupil's own idiom and even be prepared to use it to facilitate classroom instruction. What teachers *must* do is to continually emphasize that everyone needs and uses a number of different vocabularies, each serving its special purpose. The disadvantaged desperately need standard English to find and hold a job. Studies by the U.S. Department of Labor confirm this to be of vital importance.

2. Greater emphasis needs to be placed on reading, spelling, handwriting, and fundamental computational skills. Since these children have already been exposed to this knowledge for a number of years and have failed to retain it, overlearning is indicated as the most effective recourse. Without such techniques, no student can acquire even a minimum education. It is probable that the drill necessary for overlearning will be taken over by machines and tapes. Accompanying such instruction, students

need to be taught how to learn. Teachers should never take for granted that children understand simply because they ask no questions. Disadvantaged children would rather fail than expose their lack of knowledge to the teacher and classmates.

3. Cultural enrichment at the elementary level will add needed depth to the disadvantaged's impoverished background. Pupils who have never been more than a few blocks from their homes have little knowledge of the outside world and develop no motivation to learn. Films and television must be supplemented by many field trips to museums, zoos, plays, concerts, factories, farms, and sporting events. Despite the strident voices of dissidents who capture headlines and distort reality, the mainstream of society is moving steadily forward to a higher technological and cultural age. Disadvantaged children need to be brought into the contemporary scene without delay.

4. A determined effort is necessary, early in school, to raise the disadvantaged's self-esteem. Halting his succession of failures by gearing instruction to his level of achievement is only the first step. Contact between him and the school through clubs, sports, activities, counseling, and individual attention by teachers will help him achieve status. The curriculum itself can serve to instill a sense of identification and ethnic pride through cultural and racial histories. Text books that recite the achievements of men of his race are powerful ego-builders. Concrete and serious assignments that deal with real-life, rather than symbolic situations, will be most meaningful to him.

In middle school, emphasis should shift to masculinity. To young boys, school often represents a "sissy" stage, repugnant to the aggressive male, feeling his first instinctive drive for independence. Negro boys tend to pull down the scores on achievement tests in inner-city schools. Negro girls do much better. This is further proof that emotion and attitude, not race, are the crucial factors in achievement. Middle schools need male teachers, shop programs and sports. Motor activities and short term goals have most appeal to males and help hold their interest.

Middle school serves three functions. The first is remediation for those who have not attained a satisfactory level of skill for high school. In inner-city schools, where 60% of the junior high school student body reads in the lower quartile, a massive attack needs to be made on this deficiency. No dependable method of teaching reading has yet been discovered, since each individual apparently learns in discrete fashion. As yet, nothing has surpassed a combination of remedial and free reading using appropriate materials at indicated interest and maturity levels. A number of experimental projects using combined audio and visual equipment show considerable promise. A break-through is needed and may be supplied by computer-assisted instruction in connection with other methods. More will be said about these in later chapters.

The second function of middle school is preparation for an appropriate career. Those with the greatest ability (highest scores on achievement tests) should be introduced to literature, abstract mathematics, foreign language, and laboratory science to prepare them for higher education. At most, this would comprise no more than 50% of the student body. All of these students will not prove college material, but tests are so unreliable that teachers must be alert to allow no undiscovered talent to be wasted.[2] The balance of the students need training for employment by sheltered workshops or appropriate shop programs, supplemented by a general education on a level at which they can achieve.

A third function is grooming for citizenship. Disadvantaged children must comprehend that *everyone* must cooperate in a society growing more and more interdependent. They must realize that they have a vital stake in a stable society under rule of law. They need to grasp the brutal fact that, having few resources, they will be the first to suffer from any breakdown in law and order. Lastly, they need to be told frankly that intolerable injustices do exist and

---

[2] One of the *least* unsatisfactory tests for this purpose is the *Pinter Test of General Ability.*

cannot be ignored, but can be corrected by peaceful means. Violence and lawlessness can only retard progress toward equitable solutions.

Secondary school curriculum probably needs the greatest alterations. The traditional college preparatory program has little relevance for 65% to 70% of these students, since they will not be attending institutions of higher learning. It is a tragic fraud to encourage, for the sake of prestige, more than the top 30% to 35% to prepare for college. Even if admitted, experience proves that they will not survive the rigors of higher education. Middle school should have separated those with the necessary ability for college from the balance of the student body.

On the other hand, it is equally tragic not to encourage the top 30% to 35% to plan for college. The distribution of intelligence in the human race appears to consistently follow the curve of normal distribution. Any school of normal size can therefore expect 30% to 35% of its students to be capable of attending college and entering the professions or managerial level positions. These students need a strong academic program that will prepare them to enter and compete successfully with other students in any college. Finding them may be difficult, since intelligence and scholastic aptitude tests, normed on middle class children, are ill-suited to measuring the disadvantaged. However, that such intelligent and gifted children do exist everywhere is demonstrated by the fact that even in deprived neighborhoods there is a wide variation in achievement. Although achievement scores in some ghetto schools are skewed to the left, it is still possible to identify the top 35%, whether they score as high as the national norms or not. These children, with proper help, can eventually reach college. Whatever help they need, such as remedial instruction, tutoring, counseling or financial aid, must be forthcoming in any required degree. These children are the nation's hidden resources.

The remaining 65% of the secondary school students have three basic requirements:

1. To read and speak standard English and do fundamental mathematical calculations.
2. To learn a marketable skill in a technical, clerical, skilled or business field.
3. To be prepared for adult responsibilities including raising a family.

To implement the last two objectives, great flexibility is needed. Instruction should be based on the disadvantaged's own perception of their needs. Everything they learn should have use value to them. This could best be accomplished if their entire curriculum for the last two or three years of secondary school centered about the job for which they were being prepared. In short, they should believe they are being taught the skills they will need to earn a living.

Since the disadvantaged are "human smart (they relate to and understand people)," in contrast to "book smart;" are not given to self blame; are most concerned with the here and now; they need to learn a number of essential living skills to reduce the abrasiveness of their contacts with reality. Most of all, they need instruction in solving their daily problems, to include cause and effect relationship.

Many of the disadvantageds' problems center about their dealings with the establishment. What they want to learn is: (1) How to buy groceries economically, (2) how to buy a car or TV set on the installment plan, (3) how to apply for a license, (4) how to obtain an apartment in public housing, (5) how to apply for unemployment compensation, (6) where to obtain health and community services, (7) how to secure legal advice and credit, and (8) how to find and apply for a job.

Lastly, some basic psychology, sociology, and anthropology would be beneficial to enable them to understand their own behavior as well as that of their neighbors.

Improvement in instructional materials is now underway, promising a more realistic curriculum for disadvantaged and middle class alike, both in English and social studies. The content will be more accurate to eliminate false conceptions about race. The realities of everyday life will be stressed, and attainable heroes presented to all children. As Dr. James Nabrith Jr., President of Howard University pointed out: "America is not self-sufficient enough in this world of competing ideologies to risk the alienation of 2 billion colored people because of ignorant selection of materials."[3]

According to *Publisher's Weekly,* publishers have instituted production of integrated texts as early as 1960, but their adoption, so far, has not reached the neighborhood school. Book publishers will gladly furnish a listing of these books. The NEA has published for 1967-68, *The Negro American in Paperback,* a selected list, annotated for secondary school students.[4]

Other curriculum improvements may soon be evident. The U.S. Office of Education, under Title III of the Elementary and Secondary School Act of 1965, has funded 26 Central City Projects for "changes in past practices needed to meet the educational crisis in the nation's big cities."

Out of these projects will flow an increasing knowledge of the disadvantaged as well as new skills with which to attack the problem. *Central Cities Educational Projects, 1969* lists the names and addresses of those who can be contacted for further information in each city.[5]

---

[3] From a speech at NEA-PR&R Conference of Civil Rights in Education on February 8, 1967. Washington, D.C.

[4] National Education Association, 1201 16th St. N.W. Washington, D.C. Order from Publications-Sales Section (Stock No. 381-11796).

[5] *Central City Educational Projects,* 1969. U.S. Office of Education. Washington, D.C. (OE-20118)

WHY COMMUNITY INVOLVEMENT IS IMPERATIVE

Daily, the hostility of students of the inner city toward schools and teachers grows more bitter. Unless a reversal of this feeling takes place soon, an entire generation of disadvantaged children will grow up practically illiterate. This attitude reflects the feelings of parents and citizens of these communities that schools have failed to provide proper education for their children. There is ample justification for their grievances. Poverty area schools are dilapidated, text books are old, and equipment is inadequate. In many cases, instruction is poor due to rapid turnover of teachers. These conditions have resulted from deterioration of property values resulting in tax loss, as well as from the tremendous influx of rural families unfamiliar with the requirements of urban life.

A massive infusion of federal and state money is needed, but this alone will not solve the problem. A recently completed five million dollar "model" school with an inovative curriculum in Harlem has been termed a "model mess" by the New York City press because of disputes between parents and the school board. The attitude of the students of this school, mirroring the dominate attitude of adults in their community, has resulted in poor motivation to study, disrespect for school authority, and a morbid learning atmosphere in the school. On the other hand, where the will to learn exists, children can learn quite well under very adverse circumstances. In a recent gloomy report on the condition of Washington, D.C. schools, one school was found to be scoring at the national average on achievement tests despite its location in an area where the average family income does not exceed $3,000.00 annually. Similar situations may be found in other cities, plagued by disorders and low achievement level. Obviously it is the learning atmosphere of the school that determines how well children achieve. That atmosphere is a happy combination of good teachers supported by parents who have confidence in them and who convey this attitude to their children. How to achieve this condition is the crucial problem. Meyer Weinberg, Chicago City College states: "If the community as a whole were to raise its aspirations for the low-status student, including the Negro, there would be an enormous stride forward."[6]

Many educators, including the Ford Foundation, are convinced that the only solution is to turn schools back to community control. It was an attempt to implement this policy that triggered the New York City teacher's strike of 1968. The resulting damage to that city's educational system is incalculable.

Obviously, some solution must be found that will decentralize schools and relinquish a measure of control to local communities. Schools must be sensitive to local problems if they are to merit parent's support in creating a good learning atmosphere.

The initiative must come from the school administration. One blueprint, already adopted in some inner-city schools, is to employ an ethnic co-ordinator, familiar with the neighborhood, to contact churches, business men, professional people, and civic organizations. He should not make the mistake of contacting only the middle class. Contrary to some opinion, the inner-city places a high value on education, if not on the school system.

Once communication is achieved and a viable organization established, teachers and counselors should be sent out to visit parents and invite them to visit the school. Door to door contact is necessary. The traditional PTA meeting has "had it." Only open discussion and concrete proposals will stimulate genuine interest. Parents can best be persuaded

[6] Weinberg, Meyer. *Desegration Research: An Appraisal.* Phi Delta Kappa. Eighth and Union. Bloomington, Indiana 1968.

that the school belongs to them if community self-interest is respected and special group requirements met. They will demand answers to the following questions: Are both slow learners and high achievers treated as individuals with separate needs? Is discipline fairly but firmly maintained? Does the school provide needed services to all children such as books (breakfast and even clothing, if needed), dental and medical care? Is the building kept open afternoon and evening for study, sports, and recreation? Is free tutoring available? Are adult education classes scheduled? Is honest effort recognized and academic excellence encouraged? Are programs of music, painting and crafts sponsored? In short, has the school become a community center?

In some difficult situations, it may take several years of patient effort to convince parents, but their concern is great, and obvious good will must eventually meet with response. In fairly stable communities, the foregoing program can be implemented immediately. Because of rapid inflation, the needed money may not be forthcoming. Complete integration is decades away. But the education of children cannot await panaceas. Good learning atmospheres in schools are needed now. All that is required is common sense and good will on all sides.

ACHIEVING RACIAL PRIDE AND SELF-RESPECT

Nurturing racial pride is a problem schools alone cannot solve. Society as a whole must assume this responsibility for the sake of its conscience. Instilling pride is, none the less, a task schools can share to the extent of their abilities.

Anyone who has worked with disadvantaged children is stung, at times, by their self-denigration. It shows in the timid waif, who must be coaxed through the classroom door—in the tearful boy who pulls away from the well-meaning hand on his shoulders. Minority children are constantly alert for possible humiliation and condescension. They lack faith in anything better and this rancor breeds defiance, distrust, and disinterest. Charles H. Smith, Special Assistant for Urban Affairs, U.S. Office of Education states: "The black youth of the ghetto has assessed his education as irrelevant because the majority imposes its cultural values and deprecates the cultural heritage of the minority. In some schools, it has made that minority ashamed of its culture and its heritage. I do not feel that black curriculum needs are satisfied by taking 15 famous Negroes and putting them between the covers of a book . . . It seems to me that black curriculum has something to do with incorporating into history the role that the minority played in the development of this country."

He continues: "They (ghetto residents) are saying, 'come into the ghetto with a sincere commitment that you want to bring change and you'll get friendship. But in the final analyses, you must let me do it for myself. We will work together, but no longer will you do it for me. We will do it together.'"[7]

The crucial points Mr. Smith accentuates are: "Come with sincere friendship," and "We will do it together."

There are many pitfalls awaiting white teachers and administrators who grapple with the problem of educating minority students before learning to understand them. The following true incident illustrates the large gulf in communication that must be bridged.

The Case of Floyd

The boy sat rigid, defiant, in the assistant principal's office. Shabby clothes could not conceal his delicate frame, tensed now like a wire strut; nor could his scowl mar his

---

[7] Smith, Charles H. An interview. "The USOE and Urban Education." Phi Delta Kappan. Vol XL No. 1 Sept. 1968 pp 43-44.

sensitive features. In his veins flowed the blood of ancient kings.

A big, gentle man, the assistant principal was clearly on the defensive. "Floyd, I can't understand why you are always fighting. This time the boy was twice your size."

"I can take care of myself."

"Maybe—but school is no place to settle quarrels. We've tried to help you better yourself, but you're not giving us much cooperation."

"You can shove that! I know what I am—a flunky and flunkies ain't never going to better themselves—not here—especially if they're black."

The assistant principal frowned, reproving. "You're not being fair to us—or to yourself. You know everyone is alike here. Look at James! He's the first Negro ever to be elected president of the senior class. He's going to Harvard. And Kenneth, he's been admitted to the University of Nebraska on a football scholarship. We're proud of them."

"Sure—sure—you're proud—you makes pets of them. They've got brains. They make the school look good—'specially Kenneth—scoring all them touchdowns."

"You know they received no special favors," the assistant principal said, patiently. "Both boys have worked hard for everything they've got. If you worked half as hard you might get someplace also."

"You're full of——, man. I can't even read the textbooks."

The assistant principal ignored the obscenity. "You could learn. Did you ever talk to Mr. Parker, the chemistry teacher? He was born in Harlem and worked his way through Columbia University."

"Talk to him," Floyd mocked. "He don't talk to me. All them Negro teachers don't talk to me. They're white now."

The assistant principal, frowned, concerned. "I don't follow you."

Floyd's lips twisted sardonically. His face became canny now with the ancient wisdom that only races who have suffered centuries of oppression can acquire. "When you got brains—the man—he needs you. He gives you a good job. You associates with him. You begin to think white and you ain't black no more. That ain't for me, cause I'm dumb. Nobody going to give me a good job."

The assistant principal was silent, visibly dumbfounded. Finally he said, "I don't believe you're dumb. How do you know you're dumb?"

"Cause the counselor—she's always saying: 'Why don't you take the vocational course, Floyd.' You can tell her I ain't going to be no—bricklayer."

"What's wrong with being a bricklayer? Some of them make more money than I do."

"Not any dumb black ones—they don't."

The assistant principal's lips tightened with frustration. "So, maybe it is harder for you. Maybe you do have it tough. What are you going to do about it. Set on your duff and cry?"

Fury contorted Floyd's handsome face. "I ain't crying man. Ain't nobody can make me cry. I m going to get somewhere my way—not yours."

The assistant principal's craggy features hardened. "We're getting nowhere," he said sternly. "I can't have you continually breaking school rules. If you persist I'll have to—"

"Kick me out of school," Floyd taunted. "Skip it—I'm leaving right now."

After the boy had gone, the assistant principal stared out the window. He knew he hadn't handled it well. He wondered if he should have stayed with coaching.

This was not the ghetto but a fine suburban school attempting honestly to integrate. The assistant principal was a considerate, intelligent man, but Floyd had come to them in the ninth grade after eight years in a big city ghetto. He was so lacking in basic skills of reading, mathematics, and general knowledge, that his intelligence could not have been validly tested. Only a massive remedial program, coupled with patient guidance, could have equipped Floyd to succeed in this school. With the shrewdness of years of self-preservation, Floyd knew it. There was simply no place for him here.

After decades of having to play it safe for fear of offending white fellow-workers of members of the power structure, after decades of learning not to be too aggressive, or too intelligent, or too successful, minorities have developed instinctive coping techniques to preserve their integrity. Unless these techniques are recognized and dealt with tactfully by the teacher, no progress will be made. Some of the more easily identified ruses are:

1. *Putting the Teacher On*—They pretend to agree or comply with what is said but make no effort to carry it out. There is a satisfaction in thwarting authority, especially if the helpless superior does not comprehend what is happening.

2. *Being Struck Dumb*—They have a sudden, unexplained loss of memory or knowledge. Skills and information they possessed days, or even minutes before, vanish, and no amount of prompting will retrieve them.

3. *Switching the Instructor Off*—They blandly pretend not to hear what is said. When asked to take their seats or put away something they are playing with, whole classes simply ignore the request as if they had not heard.

4. *Putting Someone Down*—This usually involves sarcasm or personal abuse. They refuse to listen to persuasion or pleas for discussion. They insist on only their own point of view being heard and press it with a barrage of half-truths and irrelevancies.

These evasions are displays of independence which the weak employ against the strong. Middle class teachers are apt to become discouraged and throw up their hands in the face of such frustrations. Patience is needed to permit disadvantaged children to exercise these defenses against being "pushed around." Protection of the individual's sense of pride and power is essential to an adequate ego. Once you have earned their trust, they will no longer feel the need for such safeguards and relinquish them. It is doubtful, however, if white instructors and counselors will be very successful in ghetto schools for many years. Black students will accept advice and common sense from Negroes which would only infuriate them coming from whites. Educational task forces from the great universities have learned this to their dismay when attempting to administer projects in the Washington, D.C. and Brooklyn, N.Y. ghetto schools.

Programs to enhance racial pride must necessarily involve the entire community. At least one discerning educator has attempted to do this quite successfully. He is Sam Shepherd Jr., Director of Elementary Education of the 95% Negro Banneker District in St. Louis, Missouri. Mr. Shepherd wisely involved parents as well as pupils in the motivation process. He created a mythical character, "Mr. Achiever," who, over the radio, exhorted children to attend school regularly and work for higher achievement. Mr. Shepherd went into the neighborhood with posters carrying the same message and urged store owners to discourage loitering and truancy. Parents were furnished guides, instructing them how to help their children to study and urging them to sign a pledge that they would see that their children attended school regularly and were provided a time and place for homework.

Advertising has become so indispensable to our nation in creating favorable attitudes toward products, ideas and people, that there is good reason to believe it would also have a powerful influence in cultivating racial pride. A dignified, sensitive campaign, jointly administered by schools and minority representatives and prepared by a local university, could be used over local radio and television to trace the part minorities have played in American history. This would be piped into local schools by television so that both the children and community would view it and understand that promoting racial pride had been adopted as an educational objective.

Schools would further cooperate with this program by:

1. Displaying in their halls photos of successful minority members performing their jobs, whether as singers or bulldozer operators. As far as possible, alumni of the school should be used.

2. Work-study students or recent graduates should be in-

terviewed on the job and their stories published in local and school newspapers.

3. Minority athletes and artists should be brought to the schools to speak and perform.

4. School literature books should include the biographies of great minority leaders.

5. The entire atmosphere of the school should stress that good performance increases self-respect. Excellence in achievement, not only academic, but in all types of school work including musical, artistic, athletic, vocational, and mechanical should be recognized. Many award lists should be posted in the halls and assemblies scheduled to publicly honor recipients. Winners should receive plaques to take home to display. Exhibitions of school art and crafts should be held in the neighborhood and musical and drama groups taken into the community to perform. Opportunities to compete should extend to all levels, so that the slowest learner would have an equal chance for recognition.

It is presumptious to suggest that black, white and brown should all think alike and act alike. Some educators will complain that schools are imposing middle class culture on minority children, but disadvantaged children deserve the right to choose for themselves. If they are never taught the skills and knowledge they need to compete for jobs and recognition in our society, they have been denied this freedom of choice. If, having acquired the ability to compete successfully, they then choose to reject middle class culture, they are then, and only then, exercising the birthright that belongs to all of us.

EXPLORING THE SELF-FULFILLING PROPHECY

Education, or better yet, learning is so involved with emotion and environment that it is difficult to assess a child's true ability. Counselors who deal with test scores are continually puzzled by the contradictions between many student's apparent ability and their lack of performance. The reasons for low achievement can occasionally be found and corrected, but more often, it remains a mystery, even to the student.

One such mystery is the self-fulfilling prophecy. This can best be described as an erroneous assumption or prediction which itself elicits a type of behavior that causes the erroneous prediction to take place. Putting it simpler, if people expect a thing to happen, then they subsciously contribute toward making it happen. As an example, in a recent experiment, several teachers were told that the children in their classes were a group of slow learners. In a subsequent questionnaire, the teachers described these children as weak academically, lacking in motivation, and making very little progress. Most of the students did earn low grades. The truth, which had been withheld, was that all of the students possessed high I.Q.'s. The teachers, expecting very little from these students, had demanded very little. The students, sensing this attitude, contributed very little.

If this hypothesis is valid, the reverse effect should also take place. This means expectations of success should produce success. Apparently it does. In 1963, President Kennedy appropriated an amount of money to pay counselors to visit the home of dropouts during the summer vacation with the intent to persuade them to return to school in September. So many did return to Spingarn High School in Washington, D.C. that registrars did not have time to locate their former records. In order to get the returnees into class quickly, they simply asked the students what grade they were in when they dropped out. Many advanced themselves one or more grades. When the records were finally received, it was discovered that most were doing well in the grade they had selected for themselves. Their teachers, assuming that these students could do the work for the higher grades, had produced the appropriate response from the students.

This phenomenon is most apparent in the relationship

between schools and the disadvantaged children. It sways the judgement of both teacher and pupil. Teachers are less favorably inclined toward disadvantaged children, not only because of a vague conviction that they are not as bright, but because their teaching experience has apparently confirmed this belief. Teaching the disadvantaged is frustrating and laborious. The discouraged teacher finally yields to the rationalization of—"What are you knocking yourself out for?—you're not preparing them for Harvard." This lowering of expectation is readily apparent to disadvantaged students, who accept it without question, because it confirms their own beliefs. Most disadvantaged children do not have a high opinion of themselves or their ability to succeed. Blacks, particularly, develop a feeling of helplessness and resignation. It seems to be part of their sub-culture, communicated to them in infancy and mirroring the national prejudice. Because the path upward for them is steep and torturous, self-detraction is a logical rationalization. It excuses them from attempting the almost impossible. Teachers and students, both locked in this false symbiotic premise, cause the self-fulfilling prophecy to come true.

Happily, there is a flip side. Teachers must reassure themselves that the disadvantaged can learn as well as any children when materials and instruction are appropriate. Children, for their part, who have had small successes reinforced, will in time come to believe themselves capable of learning, and, as they approach maturity, throw off the shackles of poor self-concept. The author has, for several years, taught a class in leadership including a number of Negro students. One of the objectives of the class is to build self-esteem. On several occasions, visitors have been blindfolded and brought into the class to hear discussions and recitations. It has been impossible for these strangers to distinguish the voices of the black students from the white.

ACHIEVING DISCIPLINE AND PERSONAL SECURITY

To put this discussion into proper perspective, it is necessary to start with a flat assertion. Little learning takes place in a disorganized classroom and even less in a disorganized school. Teachers must be able to hold student's attention if they are to make assignments, explain principles, clarify misconceptions, and direct classroom procedures. Students must be able to concentrate on their assignments, free to ask questions and permitted to recite without interference. This does not imply an inflexible atmosphere or even necessarily a quiet one. It does mean that classroom activity must be under the control of the teacher at all times. In very difficult neighborhoods, several aides should be assigned to the teacher. This gives both teacher and students more security, and provides freedom to divide the class into smaller groups for individual instruction. Unruly students can thus be removed by aides and separated from those desiring to work, so that the majority will not suffer from the mistaken antics of a few. It also provides more opportunity to reshape the behavior of those few and eventually return them to the class.

In order to accomplish this goal, teachers and students must never be at the mercy of outsiders and troublemakers. In most well-staffed schools, principals and teacher's aides can come to the assistance of the classroom teacher, but in the worst-troubled spots some muscle may be needed in the form of police to patrol grounds, exits, and to investigate complaints. They should not be regular police but special duty officers trained for the job and fairly representing the ethnic groups comprising the student body. These police should operate first under the control of the principal, and secondly under a joint faculty and parents committee.

Force itself, without the consent of the students themselves, will only incite rebellion. For this reason, a democratic student government should be organized with representation on the police committee. In every school and community, there are responsible elements interested in maintaining a good school atmosphere conducive to learning. If protected, these elements will emerge. Once order has been established, a student government will itself discourage crime and unruliness so that little police action will be needed, but the better elements must be protected from reprisals in and out of school. The student government should be encouraged to set rules for student conduct, but they, themselves cannot be expected to enforce these rules. Violation of rules should be dealt with swiftly and sternly, but punishment should always emphasize rehabilitation. Expulsion from school is never a good solution.

DEALING WITH THE LANGUAGE BARRIER

The language barrier is most acute in rural and isolated areas without access to television. Having little contact with the outside world, migrant, mountain, Mexican-American, and Indian children do not even know the English names of common place objects. For communication they rely on a limited, colloquial vocabulary. Consequently, books, films and even the teacher's speech are largely incomprehensible to them. Ordinary school instruction is useless until a functional vocabulary has been acquired. Probably only a teacher of the same ethnic background could have sufficient understanding to help them. Magnifying this problem, many of these children suffer defects in sight and speech that go undiscovered because of their shyness and laconism.

Urban children who view television regularly are more sophisticated. They, at least, seem to understand what happens every day on "Dark Shadows." But even there, one study found that many disadvantaged students do not understand 30% to 50% of the words teachers use. The habit of some teachers of slurring final vowel sounds is particularly confusing to them.

Idiomatic speech is troublesome for both teacher and student, but if all a child hears in his home and community is a characteristic vernacular, this becomes his means of communication. Denying him its use leaves him perplexed and speechless. To talk of breaking a child of speaking his own language has a cruel connotation and can easily result in a speech block. Teachers forget that their inconsiderate use of middle class words is as unintelligible and amusing to the child as the child's slang is to the teacher. The "hip" vocabulary of the ghetto is limited but highly colorful and expressive. It is constantly changing and some of the following will undoubtedly find their way into our English language:

"I ast this cat did he have a job?"

"Don't jive us man. You got a nerve to come on sounding like you ain't never heard of Malcom X's black bag."

"Now ain't that a gas? Ain't that a whole trick bag?"

"Cool—now you dude's gonna tell me you ain't seen nobody gettin busted?"

Some of their talk is for the purpose of hiding their motives from parents, teachers and outsiders, but in its own picturesque way it is no more ridiculous than the pompous jargon used by psychologists and bureaucrats to say simple things. Don't correct them when they say "mouf," but do use the prime and shape technique to teach them to say "om-ow-thuh" when they are learning standard English.

Profanity and obscenity are particularly shocking to teachers who are apt to make value judgments about children without realizing that such speech is commonplace to ghetto residents. Obscenity does not have the same meaning to them as it does to middle class whites and should not be regarded by teachers as insulting. Before you teach them, stand before your mirror and say aloud to your image all the four-letter words you know (you'll be amazed at the extent of your vocabulary). Once the shock of hearing the word aloud has worn off, you'll discover you can learn to "keep your cool."

ESTABLISHING A GOOD LEARNING ATMOSPHERE

The Coleman Report[8] surprisingly indicates that there are only small differences in schools attended by Negro and white children in terms of teacher's salaries, library facilities, laboratories, school size, and provision for guidance, but that a wide discrepancy exists in the educational assets provided by the students themselves. Pupils increase their achievement when they attend a school in which most of the students come from families and environments rich in intellectual and motivational resources. The report further indicates that white middle class children can increase the achievement of disadvantaged children with no adverse effect on their own.

It would be ridiculous to conclude from this that contact with a different color skin could produce such a phenomena. The variable introduced is the attitude of the middle class child—the value he places on education which has been shaped by his favorable environment. Collectively, these individual attitudes form the learning atmosphere of the school. As a student in a school, noted for its academic excellence remarked sheepishly; "Studying is the 'in' thing

---

[8] Coleman, James S., Campbell, Ernest O., Hobson, Carol J., McPartland, James M., Modd, Alexander M., Weinfeld, Frederick D., and York, Robert L. *Equality of Educational Opportunity*. Washington, D.C. U.S. Government Printing Office. 1966.

here." When in the majority, the middle class peers of the disadvantaged student have a potent influence on his behavior. He imitates, as far as he is able, their peer culture. The middle class school provides a stimulating and exciting climate. In ghetto schools, teachers are inclined to keep instruction on the level at which most of their students work. The Phi Delta Kappa Commission on Education, Human Rights, and Responsibilities has prepared a study called *Desegregation Research: An Appraisal.*[9] Quoting from the study: "One of the implications of the Phi Delta Kappa study is that the social climate of the school constitutes an autonomous influence on aspiration."

There is some evidence that the opposite result can also take place in a school in transition. If a large majority of disadvantaged students are admitted to a middle class school, they overwhelm and retard the learning atmosphere. This should dictate caution in implementing desegration, but a judicious mix, if surveys are correct, is, at present, the best means of raising the achievement level of disadvantaged students. Where it can be accomplished intelligently, as in the Berkeley, California schools, there can be no valid argument against forthright procedure. Both white and black children are benefited by school integration. Most white children now grow up without adequate contact with or knowledge of Negroes as individuals. The same is true of black children. Our world is becoming too small and too crowded to tolerate unnatural reactions of one race toward another.

However, in larger cities and parts of the South, the concentration of Negroes quickly exhausts the possibility of mixing races. There are simply not enough middle class children to go around. The *Washington Post* for November 19, 1967, quotes Dr. John H. Fischer, president of Teacher's

---

[9] Weinberg, Meyer. *Desegregation Research: An Appraisal.* Phi Delta Kappa. Eighth and Union, Bloomington, Indiana. 1968.

College, Columbia University: "As the ghetto within the city expands into a virtual ghetto city, even the most resolute and ingenious school authorities find meaningful desegregation beyond their own capabilities." This means that in large cities, meaningful integration cannot take place within the forseeable future. Since the proper education of disadvantaged children cannot wait for panaceas without national tragedy, the problem becomes one of establishing good learning atmospheres in segregated inner-city schools.

Some methods of mixing races short of complete integration could be:

1. Schedule some classes throughout the year at nearby universities or cultural centers to be attended by both races.
2. Instead of teams from predominately black or predominately white schools competing against each other, organize integregated teams from paired schools to compete against teams from other paired schools.
3. Allow schools to contract with private organizations or individuals to teach such subjects as reading, tutorial programs or such innovative practices as talking typewriters, computer consoles, or cultural enrichment programs. Locate these centers where they would be accessible to both races and permit parents to elect to send children there for certain periods of their education.

In the meantime, ghetto schools can start to create a better learning atmosphere themselves by:

1. Enlisting community support for their programs so that parents can convey an attitude supporting good learning in the schools.
2. Training teachers and administrators to demonstrate belief in their student's ability by holding high standards of achievement before them.
3. Reorganizing the curriculum to make it more meaningful to students.
4. Maintaining a clean, well-repaired, businesslike atmosphere in the school and on the grounds.

5. Starting a campaign to raise the student's self-concept.
6. Maintaining a friendly but firm discipline in which students and faculty can respect each other's rights.

WHY THE "STORE-FRONT" SCHOOLS ARE SUCCESSFUL

One unlikely innovation that has germinated among the grime and litter of the ghetto is worth mentioning because of the fundamental simplicity of its operation. This is the "store-front" school, so called because it operates in abandoned neighborhood stores.

Foremost of the "store-front" schools are Harlem Prep in New York City, sponsored by the Urban League with support from the Ford Foundation, and CAM Academy in Chicago, which has financial backing from eight Protestant and Catholic churches. Both are designed to help dropouts from public schools who have been unable to adjust to the school setting. Harlem Prep students are selected for academic ability, and its curricula is designed to prepare them for college. CAM Academy admits all who apply. Both schools have already graduated students who are now attending colleges. Both have shown unusual ability to hold and interest "misfits." Their strength lies in their small enrollment, allowing much individual attention to be given each student, plus a lack of rigid structure, permitting great flexibility in teaching. They have another salutary quality not so easily defined. It is the warmth and acceptance of the student as an individual with the right to learn or not to learn as he sees fit. In a sense they are throw-backs to the "little red school house" where students all aided one another and the individual was prized for himself—not for his spelling.

HOW SUCCESSFUL IS INTEGRATION?

Studies by the United States Commission on Civil Rights show two pertinent facts:

1. In spite of the efforts being made to desegrate schools throughout the nation, the number of Negro students in segregated schools is increasing.
2. Compensatory education as presently organized has failed for two reasons: (a) It is conducted in a racially isolated framework, and (b) it is inadequately financed.[10]

There can be no argument with the premise that complete integration must always be the national goal, but the wide gap between principle and reality remains a thorny issue. To establish artificial boundaries to maintain segregation was an odious practice, but applying the same reasoning, to establish boundaries for the sole purpose of maintaining some ideal mixture of the races seems ill-conceived. It often results in creating all-black schools that once held some white students.

Bussing students to outlying areas can have equally disastrous consequences. At best, it can result in creating "in" groups and "out" groups in the school. Human beings are territorially oriented. The further they are removed from familiar surroundings, the more uneasy they become. Disadvantaged students are insecure enough without increasing their vulnerability. Such a hasty political decision was to blame for changing the Washington, D.C. schools from 60% black to 90% black in a single decade.

The Phi Delta Kappa Commission on Education, Human Rights, and Responsibilities has prepared a report[11]

---

[10] United States Commission on Civil Rights. Racial Isolation in the Public Schools. 2 vols. U.S. Government Printing Office. Washington, D.C. 1967.

[11] Weinberg, Meyer. *Desegregation Research: An Appraisal* Phi Delta Kappa. Eighth and Union, Bloomington, Indiana. 1968.

which includes the Coleman Report,[12] a study commissioned by the United States Department of Education. The Phi Delta Kappa report is an exhaustive review of research on the effects of school desegregation. Some of its principal conclusions are:

1. "Academic achievement rises as the minority child in the majority white school learns more while the white child continues to learn at his accustomed rate."
2. "Negro aspirations, already high, are positively affected; self-esteem rises; and self-acceptance as a Negro grows."
3. "The effects of desegregation on Negro Americans are evident and the support the Negro community lends to desegregation is widespread and perhaps growing."

Two other plans for integregating schools have received national attention. One is the education park, which would be centrally-located complexes housing up to 15,000 students of various grades including up to K-12. Pittsburgh, Pennsylvania, Syracuse and New York, New York have such plans in various stages of development backed by federal support. They would be located so that a mixture of races could be achieved by bussing both races equal distances. There are many drawbacks to these projects, not the least being that there is no assurance that they will not become giant de facto segregated institutions in the future.

A more modest proposal has been developed in Mount Vernon, New York to permit some desegregation and at the same time preserve the neighborhood school. A child's academy would be constructed and all children bussed there for two hours a day. The remainder of the day would be spent in neighborhood schools. This seems practical but is being attacked by both sides of the civil rights issue.[13]

---

[12] Coleman, James S. et al. *Equality of Educational Opportunity.* U.S. Government Printing Office, Washington, D.C. 1966.

[13] For further information on desegregation consult: Education Parks, U.S. Commission on Civil Rights. Clearinghouse Publication No. 9. U.S. Government Printing Office Washington. D.C.

MOTIVATING THE DISADVANTAGED
WITH IMMEDIATE REINFORCEMENT

We suggest that there is no more subtle student of American society than the black man, and when he suspects that he is called to a race where there is no prize, he simply declines to run.

— From *Black Rage* by
William H. Grier & Price M. Cobbs
(Basic Books, Inc., New York, 1968)

Too often have schools offered no prize to students, black or white, who are consigned to the bottom of the scholastic heap; but the black student suffers from an additional handicap. Even when he runs, he finds that the prize is not for him. Only in the past few years have colleges sought the Negro student with good grades, and he still finds grudging acceptance in graduate and professional schools. Only recently are white collar jobs available. The non-academic Negro's high school diploma was worthless in the job market, and unions barred him from skilled jobs, even when he was qualified. If psychologists characterize him as "now" oriented, this is a completely logical consequence of his experience. A bleak future does not motivate sacrifices to obtain it. White middle class children are brought up with the idea of deferring present gratification in favor of greater benefits in the future. They can study for many years with the almost-certain assurance that this sacrifice will eventually pay off. For the Negro, no such rosy portend exists. A small crack is at last appearing in the barred door. The *Occupational Outlook Quarterly* for summer 1969, published by the U.S. Department of Labor states: "The Negro (college) graduate who has reasonably good grades will have no trouble finding a job." But this fact has not yet penetrated into the ghetto, and until it does, the disadvantaged student will need more tangible rewards to motivate him.

This does not mean that he places small value on intrinsic rewards. He receives the same satisfaction from a job well done as whites. He responds to conventional school rewards such as praise and high grades in the same manner as white children. But he is suspicious of being "put on" and this makes him a poor starter. It would be wrong to pin such a label on all disadvantaged children. Some work diligently, but not the hard core—the dropout—the gang member. He can only be motivated by immediate and meaningful compensation. Food, drinks and money are the most practical, although special privileges and prestige have also proven effective. Once he has started to achieve and knows it, he will begin to respond to conventional school rewards. He has too much pride to continue to be bribed for self-improvement.

In the final analysis, a way must be found to provide the high school graduate a self-respecting job, commensurate with his ability. Studies have shown that the dropout rate closely parallels the unemployment rate in the big cities. Schools must work more closely with state and federal employment agencies or get into the job placement business themselves. When we can guarantee everyone who is willing to prepare himself for it a job, achievement in the ghetto schools will begin to rise in spite of all other handicaps.

TRAINING TEACHERS FOR THE INNER CITY SCHOOLS

Procurement of teachers for the inner city is in shambles. The turnover in Washington, D.C. schools is from 35% to 50% each year. Sometimes children hardly learn the name of the teacher before she is replaced by a substitute who is in turn replaced by another teacher, and so on in a confusing migration. Why this frantic exodus? In Chicago schools, for example, all beginning teachers start in lower class schools, and most transfer as soon as they acquire seniority. Thus, the least prepared, the least secure, the least experienced are placed in the most difficult jobs. (This is not meant to disparage the very few dedicated teachers who do stay and perform miracles.)

Teaching is the one profession where skills are acquired mostly by trial and error. The gap between college theory and the actual classroom situation is so wide, it often seems that professor and student are not on the same channel. In-service training is one of the biggest hoaxes in education, being occupied mostly with trivia and irrevelancies. In-service is a ritual for the superintendent's report. Since the teacher is the lesson, some start must be made to procure skilled and self-confident teachers for the ghetto schools.

Industry, when faced with the problem of finding personnel for unattractive jobs, does not hesitate to offer increased wages and privileges. Ghetto teachers should, therefore, be offered a supplement plus several short vacations a year to recuperate from mental strain. Moreover, they should be paid to attend classes that update their skills every two years. Extra pay is not the only requirement for recruiting proper teachers for the ghetto, since that would also attract spongers, interested in the pay but not in the hard work. New teachers should be carefully screened. Young people with ideals and a desire to make a contribution to society abound on our campuses. Not the wide-eyed pseudo-intellectuals who seem to feel that enthusiasm is a substitute for careful preparation, but sincere and responsible students. It is to this group that recruitment should be directed. Such prospects can be offered three year probationary contractual internships, extending through their senior year and two years of actual teaching. Opportunities for promotion without moving into administration should include specialist training in reading—teaching English as a second language—speech therapy—counseling—and new techniques connected with audio-visual and computer assisted instruction. Another promotional opportunity would be to head a team of teacher's aides. The foregoing suggestions would undoubtedly be expensive, but the cost could be materially reduced by a wider use of teacher's aides who would perform the following functions:

1. Individualize instruction.
2. Perform clerical duties.
3. Take over habitual troublemakers.
4. Provide support and security to the teacher thereby increasing her margin of safety as well as permit more planning.

Training teachers for the ghetto must be taken off the campus and into the communities which will provide a laboratory for study. A teacher's training center, operated under contract with a local university, would be located near schools to which teachers would be assigned. The staff of the center would also do research and develop new methods of instruction. They would teach, consult with school and community officials, investigate new ideas, and use the local schools as a laboratory for training both new and experienced teachers by demonstrating how new procedures would actually work in the classroom.

Since beginners in any field are initially insecure, two or three student teachers should be assigned together for training and eventually to the same schools for mutual support. During their senior year, they would be under the supervision of an experienced teacher from the school to which they would be assigned to guide and integrate them into the faculty. Hunter College in New York City has already initiated a similar plan. By visiting families of their future students these teachers would acquire genuine understanding of their children's problems. They would realize, for example:

1. Johnny may be tardy because there is no clock in the house.
2. Ann's dress may often be dirty because her mother washes for nine by hand without hot water.
3. That moral and immoral do not have the same meaning to her students as they do to her.
4. That although life is harsh and family structure unstable, genuine warmth and affection does exist between parents and children of the ghetto.[14]

---

[14] Much of the above is from the pamphlet *Inner City Schools and the Beginning Teacher.* Levine, Daniel U. and Doll, Russell C. Phi Delta Kappa. Eighth and Union, Bloomington, Indiana. 1966 p 9.

chapter 5

Adjusting the
Middle School Program
to the Slow Learner

Middle school is the more popular term used today to describe the separate schools housing the seventh and eighth grades. It is used interchangeably here with the term junior high school which commonly includes the ninth grade as well. Its existence is based on the educational theory (which may or not be true) that budding adolescence, being a time of rapid change and uncertainty, requires a unique setting. No longer being a child, the young adolescent should be separated from elementary children; but still being immature, needs time to prepare for association with high school pupils. The fact that there can be a spread of as much as four years between chronological age and maturity level seems to nullify this premise almost immediately. However, since *how* the student is taught, not *where* he is being taught makes the difference in his learning, the middle school setting, being a hybrid of elementary and high school, seems as appropriate as any and does allow time for exploration, growth and adjustment before plunging into preparation for young adulthood. The main criticism directed toward the middle school is that it soon becomes a kingdom in its own. In actual practice, little coordination exists between the elementary, middle and high schools. Consequently, the student is not prepared for either change. It is principally this fault with which this chapter is concerned. Slow learners need a smoothly coordinated program from K to 12 to avoid setbacks, discouragements and further failure. If a slow learner has been the beneficiary of an enlightened program in elementary school and has benefited through restored confidence in his ability, a grave injustice has been committed if he suddenly finds himself confronted with a hostile or indifferent attitude in middle school. Confusion, bitterness and resignation will be the inevitable result.

INTEGRATING THE PROGRAM WITH THE ELEMENTARY AND HIGH SCHOOLS

Although ornamented with pretentious educational theories, the pragmatic function of middle school is still to prepare the student for high school. Since individual differences grow more pronounced as the child matures, the need for tailored schedules to accommodate slow learners increases. Gains from elementary school must be preserved and expanded, while deficiencies must be repaired. These aims can only be accomplished if the true status of each student is known. For this purpose, middle schools need adequate numbers of trained counselors. Prior to graduation, these counselors should visit the feeder schools and interview each sixth grader as well as his teachers. After a study of the student's record, the counselor is prepared to sit down with him and plan his middle school schedule. Elementary school records will provide many clues to the individual's abilities, needs and interests.

After seven years of schooling, it should be apparent to the genuine slow learner and his parents that a four year college is beyond his capacity but that realistic education and training can, none the less, place him in a good job. He needs to be continued in a program of English, mathematics, social studies, science, and physical education at a level which he will find successful. Concurrent with this, exploration should be initiated in such vocational fields as crafts, technical, and business training. This career reconnaissance will provide him with the necessary feedback to enable him to make his own selection of vocational education when he reaches high school. If he feels he is headed toward a definite goal, his education will be far more meaningful to him. The disadvantaged and others, still far below seventh grade level, need massive remediation and tutorial assistance.

The emotionally-disturbed underachiever still remains the greatest enigma. If his test scores indicate that he has the ability to attend college, he should be entered in an academic program supplemented by intensive counseling in an effort to challenge him. Should his grades, however, show no improvement, it is better to move him back with the slow learners than risk failure.

Many slow learners will show, during elementary school, skill in such areas as art, music, drama, mechanics, and even latent creativity. These students should be given an opportunity to develop such aptitudes in more depth during middle school. This will provide them with much needed success and even portend a possible career.

Logically, middle school should be nongraded, since gifted students may require only a year to prepare them for high school, while the slow learner needs two, and in cases of severe retardation, three years. If he is retained, it must be without failing him. Establishing a nongraded Language Development Center and a Mathematics Laboratory will provide the necessary apparatus for avoiding failure.

The slow learner's exit from middle school should be prepared even more carefully so that his entrance into high school is smoothly paved. Prior to his graduation, counselors from high school should visit the middle school. The accumulated knowledge in each student's folder from both elementary and middle school will help them to wisely assist each student in planning his high school program.

IDENTIFYING STUDENTS WITH SPECIAL NEEDS

Middle school is probably the last opportunity schools will have to intervene in the student's life with much success. Character traits and defense mechanisms become self-sustaining at this stage. All children in their early teens have rapidly shifting behavior patterns so that teachers and counselors overlook the child with serious problems. Symptoms to look for are: excessive absences and tardies, class skipping, and fighting. These are unmistakable signs of deep-seated emotional problems. Home visitation is a must and inevitably throws light on the causative factors.

A second group of students in need of help are the small, child-like elfs, still too immature to compete with their overpowering classmates. Growth will eventually solve their problems, but, in the meantime, they need to be sheltered by a friendly and tactful adult.

New students from other school systems need to be given batteries of tests by the guidance department to determine their level of placement. The California Achievement Tests and the Iowa Tests of Educational Development are useful for this purpose. In the eighth grade, the Differential Aptitude Tests are invaluable for all middle school students and are fairly reliable. They quickly denote discrepencies between verbal and numerical aptitudes. This information is highly valuable in planning high school schedules and making career choices. The Differential Aptitude Test furnishes other useful items of intelligence to teachers and counselors. If a child's abstract intelligence score is much higher than either his verbal or numerical scores, it indicates he has greater ability than his performance signifies and needs remediation in English and mathematics. The space score on the DAT is a trustworthy predictor of artistic talent and points toward a possible career in architecture, design, or art.

Students who enter the school system late in the elementary school, as well as those whose performance shows a distinct change in pattern, need to be retested to prevent them from being frozen in any definite category. It cannot be emphasized too strongly that thorough knowledge of the individual by the guidance department is vital to prevent teachers from operating in the dark.

USING THE LANGUAGE DEVELOPMENT CENTER— THE MATHEMATICS LABORATORY—TUTORIAL ASSISTANCE

Approximately 25% of the student body in middle school will be in need of remedial assistance in varying degrees. Middle schools must develop a strategy flexible enough to provide these pupils with individual assistance rather than simply rely on the archaic solution of failure. For this purpose, the following is suggested:

1. A nongraded language development center, operated by a reading specialist and one or more English teachers, and assisted by a number of teacher's aides should be established. It should be equipped with teaching machines in carrels, overhead projectors, tape recorders, phonographs, controlled readers, tachistoscopes, movie projectors, and a television set. It should have a reading center with a voluminous library of paperback books and magazines on numerous levels of difficulty and interest. This development center would operate at multi-levels of difficulty in areas such

as reading, listening, writing, and speech. A child should be able to spend from a few months to more than a year in any level he requires. He should spend as many hours of the day as deemed necessary in the center, and, most important, he should be able to spend his entire middle school career in the center without being failed. Instruction should be conducted in small or large groups, depending on whatever he is being taught, under the supervision of the teacher's aides. Some students will work on spelling and vocabulary using the machines in the carrels, some will receive instruction in reading with the controlled reader, while others are taught speech and listening by tape recorders, movie projectors or TV. Each day, a free reading period in the center's library should be scheduled and books checked out to take home.

More important than the machines to provide individual instruction will be the tutorial assistance supplied each child by the teacher's aides. Children such as these are incapable of sufficient self-discipline to learn properly without close supervision. A classroom teacher with 25 or more students cannot provide such support in a 50 minute period.

Diagnostic tests would be given at frequent periods to adjust levels of instruction, and grades would be assigned on the basis of the child's progress after an individual conference, so that the student is aware of his own progress. Students who interrupt instruction or disturb classmates would be removed to private areas by a teacher's aide until they are capable of self-control. The development center's teachers, free of discipline problems, will have time to teach, plan, direct, diagnose, and evaluate.

2. A nongraded mathematics laboratory would be staffed by one or more mathematics teachers assisted by several teacher's aides. It would also be equipped with teaching machines in carrels, overhead and opaque projectors, film strips, controlled readers, tape recorders, and movie projectors. In addition it would have remote terminals for computers, measuring devices, geobands, electric calculators, mathematical equipment, models, games, puzzles, and construction equipment for individual student use.

The mathematics laboratory is relatively new and more will be said about it in a succeeding chapter. It is ideally suited to slow learners and those having difficulty with numerical skills. It permits a concrete, rather than symbolical approach. Students can handle and manipulate mathematical models that formerly they were required to visualize from the printed page or from diagrams on the chalk board. It provides opportunity for them to see mathe-matical representation in several forms and through several senses. Its primary goal is to change the student's attitude toward mathe-matics and to make it meaningful to him. He becomes an active participant rather than a passive learner.

The mathematics laboratory will probably need even more teacher's aides since tutorial assistance must be almost on a one-to-one basis. The Job Corps Training Centers have found that instruction for remedial students must be almost entirely individu-alized.

Operation would be quite similar to the language development center, except that one period a day would probably be as long as a slow learner could be challenged. He should, however, spend as much of his middle school sojourn in the laboratory as deemed necessary without being failed.

HOW COUNSELORS CAN ASSIST
THE MIDDLE SCHOOL PROGRAM

Counselors in middle school, where they exist at all, usually have a counseling load of from 600 to 800 or more counselees. This dilutes their services almost to the point of impotency, yet middle school is the turning point in a child's educational experience, during which he requires consider-able guidance and support. In elementary schools he has been accustomed to one teacher for a large portion of the day, a surrogate parent, so to speak. This teacher, in turn, has only to shepherd thirty to forty pupils. She can learn to understand, guide and even to love them. The child, for his part, enjoys a feeling of security in her room comparable to his own home.

On entering middle school, even where combination classes are taught by the same person, a student is asked to adjust to four different instructors each day. The teacher herself is required to learn the idiosyncrasies of from 100 to 150 new charges. She is fortunate to learn all of their names by mid-term. Thus, children are left anchorless during a crucial period. Counselors, if permitted, could do much to fill this gap. It is disheartening to find that only a small fraction of middle school children are even aware that counselors can be turned to for support and advice. In particular need are those immature children, less ready than their classmates to stretch their wings. For the confident and aggressive child, starting middle school can be an exhilarating adventure, but for slow learners, already fearful and discouraged, the experience is often traumatic. The following true episode illustrates the role a counselor can play in boosting slow learners over the hurdle.

The Case of Emma Cobb

The counselor often accompanied 7th graders on field trips. He had found young students to be wary and constrained when first visiting his office. Viewing them in the classroom was entering an artificial world, but a field trip was a holiday and students reacted with a spontaneity that revealed insights into their behavior. He first noticed Emma, who was seated alone several rows ahead of him, because she clutched in her hand two $1.00 bills. She was noticeably quiet, gazing solemnly out the bus window. He noted that her dress was a hand-me-down, and that she wore battered sneakers, contrasting shabbily with the other children. Having no purse, she was evidently reluctant to trust the precious bills to her flimsy dress pocket. The rigid set of her torso, dumpy with baby fat, indicated her apprehension. The bus was alive with the boisterous shouting, giggling and squirming of young teens, but Emma took no part.

The counselor moved up to the vacant seat beside her and said, "Hello."

She glanced at him, then turned quickly to the window again.

"My name is Mr. Bryant," he volunteered, "what's your name?"

"Emma," she said, without looking at him.

"Would you like me to hold your money?" he offered, "you might lose it."

Emma shook her head.

"Why did you bring so much money on this trip?"

"Miss Harvey said we might stop at a roadside stand to buy drinks, so Mama gave me two dollars."

The counselor nodded his head with silent admiration for Mama who must have made a grand gesture she probably couldn't afford so that Emma could hold up her head.

The conversation came to an end as the bus reached its first destination, a model farm. The children tumbled out to be taken on a tour of the fields and barns. Miss Harvey went first to point out items of interest, while the counselor brought up the rear. The walk was long, and toward the end, Mr. Bryant came upon Emma seated at the foot of a hill.

"What's wrong?" he asked.

"I can't keep up. My side hurts."

He squatted beside her. "We'll rest and then you take my hand."

When, at last, they reached the top of the hill, she did not withdraw her hand until they were back on the bus.

The second goal of the trip was a guided tour of the FBI Building in Washington, D.C., ending at the firing range. It was an exciting experience for the children, who crowded about the guide, deluging him with questions. Only Emma stayed close to Mr. Bryant. When the agent fired the sub-machine gun, Emma gasped and trembled.

Mr. Bryant put his arm about her shoulders. "It scares me too," he said.

Sure enough, Miss Harvey, an understanding teacher, stopped for drinks on the way home. Emma returned to the bus with two bottles.

"I bought you a drink," she told Mr. Bryant. He shuddered inwardly at the syrupy beverage (he was watching his waist line) but drank it bravely.

The next week, Mr. Bryant visited Emma's home. The situation could hardly have been worse. Her father was unknown and her mother's occupation somewhat vague. The house was run down with several broken windows, which Emma's mother attributed to neighborhood vandals.

"Emma's always been small for her age," the mother told Mr. Bryant. "I was right poorly when I carried her."

The next day, Mr. Bryant contacted the Family Welfare Service and requested them to look into the circumstances. He then studied Emma's school situation. It was in shambles. Being a slow learner, the change from elementary school had overwhelmed her. Her teachers reported that "she was no problem," but did not participate in class. Most of her papers were undecipherable.

Mr. Bryant managed to see her almost daily for most of the school year. He reorganized her note books, secured tutors and changed some of her teachers. To her credit, Emma struggled doggedly, and, except for mathematics, managed to pass everything at the end of the 7th grade.

When she returned in the fall of the 8th grade, she had magically lost her baby fat. Mr. Bryant noticed her giggling with two boys and knew she was ready to be weaned. He was glad of it, because she had taken to eating chocolate candy bars in his office while he was trying to skip the high calorie school lunches.

Counselors can work very successfully with small groups of slow learners. In order not to sound ominous, these groups can be called "discussion groups" or "analysis groups". To allow for absentees, they should consist of ten or twelve students and meet once a week for eight to ten weeks or longer. Careful selection will facilitate the progress of the group. Not more than one possible leader should be included lest a struggle for dominance occupy too much of the group's time. Nor more than one dedicated attention-seeker should be included. Two or more will vie with each other for the limelight. Include enough better-adjusted children to support each other and they will supply most of the sensible dialogue needed. These students will be your sounding board and exert beneficial influence on the others. A successful group requires careful ground work by a series of individual conferences. The counselor must know each group member's personality and behavior pattern before he forms the group. In addition, he must have established some rapport with each individual or he will encounter more hostility than he can cope with.

The object of the discussions should be motivational. This goal can best be arrived at by allowing children to ventilate their grievances and emotions about school, about teachers, or about any strong feelings they may have. The counselor constantly assures them they are free to express their opinions since nothing they say is ever repeated outside the group. He warns the group that anyone who violates this rule will be immediately dropped. He explains that he is not there as a teacher but as a group member. He is entitled to his opinions just as they are but can be challenged like any other member. A second caution he must lay down is to avoid personal or insulting remarks about each other or their families. Other than that, they are free to express dislikes and differences. He will never be able to avoid some bitter exchanges but must judge for himself how far to let them go before intervening. He is never judgmental but does not necessarily agree with everything said. His job is to question, to reflect back what is said for clarification. He keeps the discussion going and attempts tactfully to involve silent members. When he feels the discussion has strayed too far afield, he returns it to the topic he wishes to develop. As long as the discussion is progressing, he takes no part. He can defend himself when attacked, but it is good technique to ask the group why they think his critic felt the need for such an attack. Reflecting back for group consideration all irrational statements is the real purpose of the group and provides beneficial therapy. One caution needs to be emphasized. No spectacular modification in behavior should be anticipated. It takes time and maturity to reverse emotional attitudes that have been years in formation. Changes are often noticeable during the group's existence, but results are sometimes evident only years later.

The following are actual transcripts of group discussions which illustrate what can be expected. The first is the third session of a group of six boys and four girls, all 8th graders:

Counselor.	"Everyone have fun this week-end?"
Chorus.	"Nah! Too short! It was a drag! I didn't!"
Janice.	"I did. I had a party. It was my birthday."
Counselor.	"Happy birthday. How old—now—are you?"
Janice.	"Thirteen."
Counselor.	"Really! A teen-ager, eh?"
Phillip.	"Big deal. I'll be fifteen in two weeks."
Janice.	"I wouldn't brag. You're still in the 8th grade."
Counselor.	"Let's get started—now—where did we stop last week? (pause) I believe we agreed that schools and teachers can't make you learn. Isn't that right? (pause) Can they make you learn?"
James.	"Sure."
Irene.	"He's crazy—he always talks crazy—he gotta show off."
James.	"They makes you learn, cause they hits you—they gotta big stick an they wham you on your head."
Irene.	"Somebody ought to wham your head. He makes me sick."
Counselor.	"How about you, Ava? Can teachers make you learn?"
Ava.	(giggles) "Ain't nobody can make me do anything. My mother—she say I got a nob (sic) head."
James.	"You gotta knot head. It look like a board."
Ava.	"You shut up fore I smack you in the mouth. He thinks he's so smart."
Counselor.	"How about you, Helen. Can teachers make you learn?"
Helen.	"Not unless I want to."
Counselor.	"You have to want to learn—is that right?"
Jack.	"Some teachers make you want to learn."
Counselor.	"How do they do that?"
Jack.	"Mr. Jones showed me how to clean my aquarium."
Irene.	"Yea—he's real cool. He put all the baby guppies in another tank so—so the big fish wouldn't eat 'em."
Phillip.	"That ain't nothing. Everybody knows that."

Counselor. "How about other teachers—do they make you want to learn?"

Janice. "Old Mrs. Burns don't. She gave us thirty math problems we gotta do by Friday."

Phillip. "Yea, she's mean."

Counselor. "You think she does that because she doesn't like you?"

Janice. "She don't like me."

Irene. "Me neither."

Counselor. "Why do you think she doesn't like you?"

Janice. (giggles) "Cause I don't do no work."

Counselor. "Do you think she would like you if you—uh did your work—uh—like she said?"

Chorus. "Nah—she's mean."

Irene. "She hates kids."

Counselor. "So you all think Mrs. Burns gives you school work because she hates you?"

Helen. "Well—I don't think she hates kids—but she gives us a lot of homework."

Jack. "She don't explain nothing. When somebody asks her a question she says 'You weren't paying attention when I explained!'"

Helen. "You weren't paying attention today—you were looking in your wallet."

Jack. "When?"

Helen. "When she called on you.'

Counselor. "You mean Mrs. Burns just gives you work without showing you—uh—how to do it?"

Kenneth. "She shows us. Some kids just goof off and don't listen—that's all."

Irene. "You just saying that cause you makes good grades—that's all. You her lambie-pie."

Helen. "That's not so. Mrs. Burns made Kenneth stay after school yesterday."

Ava. "You saying that cause you likes him—you his—"
(The word is indistinct)

Chorus. (giggles and laughs)

Helen. "I am not."

Barry. "Kenneth makes good grades because he likes math. I hate math."

Counselor. "You mean you make good grades if you like a subjec and poor grades if you don't like it?"

Chorus.   "Yea."
Irene.   "I make good grades in music cause I like to sing."
Counselor. "You are saying then, its your feeling about the subject and not the teacher that makes you want to learn."

There is a long pause as they think this over. Note that Buford, the sixth boy, has been silent.

The following is the tenth session. Buford has dropped out of the group, although the counselor continues to see him individually. The frank give and take of the group is probably too threatening to Buford. His mother is over-protective and does not approve of him being in the group. Buford says the other kids are dumb.

Counselor. "Why is everyone so quiet today?"
Irene.   "We's tired of talking—cepting James—he got a big mouth."
James.   "You got big feet. When you knocks on the door knock—knock—knock—somebody say, 'feet come on in.'"
Counselor. "I thought you had agreed to be friends?"
James.   "Aw—she's all right—except she got big feet."
Counselor. "Well, we have to start somewhere. I think we agreed last week that school can be a drag, but you still need it."
Phillip.   "I don't—I can work for my Dad."
Counselor. "You mean your father wants you to quit school and go to work for him?"
Phillip.   "Nah—he won't let me quit. He says I gotta amount to something."
Janice.   "You ain't gonna amount to nothing less than you study."
Phillip.   "Listen to who's talking. I ain't never seen you study."
Janice.   "I study—when I feel like it."
Counselor. "When you do study, what makes you feel like it?"
Janice.   "I don't know—its—well—like yesterday. Mrs. Forman, the home ec teacher, she says I got a gift for cooking. She says maybe I could be a cook or dietitian if I made better grades."
Helen.   "My mother's a nurse. I'm going to be one too."
Kenneth.   "I'd like to work a computer."

Counselor. "Barry, how about you?"
Barry. "My father says I'm going to be a bum.'
Phillip. "Yea—me too."
Irene. "I'm going to be a model."
Counselor. "Those are fine goals. How do you plan to achieve them?"
(There is a long pause while they think.)
Helen. "Stay in school?"
Counselor. "How about you, James, are you going to stay in school?"
James. "I guess so—but it's a drag."

The insights that this group has tentatively explored are not difficult to discern. Note that between the third and tenth session more group cohesiveness has developed and there has been a slight growth in realism. They have apparently accepted school as a necessity and are giving some thought to why they are in school.

HOW VALUABLE ARE HOME VISITATIONS?

Counselors can often assist slow learners by home visitations. Excessive absences and tardies furnish a legitimate excuse for contacting parents. The results occasionally illuminate starkly what might have been passed off by the school as inexcusable or deliquent behavior. It is not unusual to find the child has no shoes or other necessary garments to wear or that she is required to mind infant siblings for a habitually weak or ailing mother. These situations can be corrected, but many poignant cases have no cure. Anti-social behavior by a boy whose father is unknown, whose mother is an alcoholic and whose two older brothers are in jail becomes understandable, yet the counselor possesses no magic remedy. All he can do is to explain the situation to teachers and administrators, endeavoring to soften the school's attitude and obtain yet another pardon in the desperate hope that a few more months of school will be better than the vicious basic training of the streets.

MOTIVATING THE "HARD-CORE" WITH PRE-EMPLOYMENT TRAINING

Students age 12 and 13 are too young to obtain regular employment due to labor laws, yet there are certain jobs they can hold without endangering their health. Moreover, these jobs provide valuable training for the future when they will be able to obtain work permits. The "hard-core" behavior problem age 12 to 15 is difficult for the middle school to reach unless a meaningful reinforcement can be offered, sufficiently effective to guarantee conformity to school rules. Earning small amounts of money can have this impact. Performing a useful task which resembles or simulates adult behavior bolsters the egos of slow learners. Often, for the first time in their lives, other children envy them.

It is quite feasible for middle schools to establish sheltered workshops for this purpose. It has been done in the Quincy Illinois public schools with the aid of the U.S. Office of Education and Southern Illinois University.[1] Employment can be offered through the following projects.

1. A school store managed by a teacher but employing students.
2. Cafeteria and custodial help in the school.
3. Contract work performed in the school, such as stuffing and addressing envelopes.
4. Making and selling artificial flowers and costume jewelry.
5. Leasing a nearby filling station to be operated on a non-profit basis by an experienced adult manager as a training station for students.

---

[1] Matthews, Charles V. and Roan, John E. *Deliquency Study and Youth Development Project.* Southern Illinois University June 1966.

SAMPLE PROGRAMS

Slow learners in middle school progress most when they are involved in the learning process. This does not imply that they should be asked, "What do you want to learn?" or "What shall we do today?" These are foolish questions and evoke foolish responses. Moreover, student planning can be carried to a ridiculous extreme. Common sense should dictate to the teacher what can be expected of students and what their limitations are. Children's education should never be sacrificed to any shibboleth. Valuable insights, however, can be obtained by teachers who listen to slow learner's responses to the question, "What are you interested in?" Teachers should then use their own knowledge of the world to build meaningful lessons upon the student's suggestions.

In the classroom, combine as many of the senses as possible during instruction. Slow learners quickly tune out lectures or long presentations, so get to the point simply and briefly—then let them do it. The problems used must be plain, concrete and carefully structured. Slow learners must work with their hands as well as their minds. The following are suggestions that have been successfully tried but are meant only to inspire the teacher's ingenuity.

Social Studies

Slow learners need knowledge in three areas in order to function well in contemporary society:

1. *Other Races and Peoples of the Earth*—This probably can best be taught with films, film strips, tapes, and records. These items are in plentiful supply.

2. *Their Own Community*—Trace its growth to the present, using old maps and photographs. They like to draw and embellish maps or construct replicas. The community's history can be reconstructed through visits to museums, old houses, and old sections of the town. They

will enjoy drawing old costumes, buildings, tools, and vehicles. They will write and act in plays depicting historical events and like to play historical characters.

The modern community can be made to come to life with a map and telephone directory. Have them locate on the map such essential services as government buildings, police and fire stations, hospitals and schools, bus and railroad terminals. They need to comprehend the complexities of modern society by visiting banks, factories, road and building construction sites, airports, universities, courts and city councils in session, and research laboratories. Once again, writing scenes and role playing important characters such as the mayor, or chief of police brings home to them the significance of what they have seen. Allow them to use the tape recorder and overhead projector for this purpose.

3. *Current Events*—Television can play a large role, but daily newspapers and such magazines as *Scope*[2], which can be read by slow learners, are very useful for bulletin boards and furnish material for role playing.

Science

Most science testbooks are too difficult for them to read, but they are fascinated by living things. Some suggestions are:

1. *A Bug Board*—Have them bring in insects they capture, classify them, and mount on a board.

2. *Cages of Mice, Guinea Pigs, Hamsters, Rabbits, Frogs and Reptiles*—These are very popular with students who will eagerly volunteer to feed and care for them. Many biological principles can be taught through this interest.

3. *Aquariums of Fish, Snails, etc.*—The teacher can make fast friends by having students bring in a jar in order to take home a fish and water plants of their own. Let them use their jars to experiment with the carbon dioxide-oxygen exchange. These can also teach valuable lessons in pollution.

4. *Planting Seeds*—If various soils and schedules of

---

[2]Order from Scholastic Scope 902 Sylvan Ave. Englewood Cliffs New Jersey. 07632.

watering and fertilizing are carried out they will discover many facts about vegetation growth for themselves. Combine this with a terrarium for frogs and terrapins.

5. *Typing Their Own Blood*—Do not press those who are too timid for this exercise.

6. *Using the Microscope*—Let them study their own skin and hair as well as plants, animals and microscopic life found in their own neighborhood.

7. *Incubating Chicken Eggs*—Open these at several day intervals to illustrate the growth of the embryo. Each child should have his own egg.

COMPREHENSIVE PROGRAMS

A demonstration program conducted with slow learning, socially-alienated students for grades 7 to 12 has been conducted by t(ffl Quincy, Illinois, public schools in association with Southern Illinois University under contract to the U.S. Office of Education. Complete texts of the study and curriculum can be obtained on microfilm.[3] Additional suggestions for teachers can be found in the pamphlet, *Educating Disadvantaged Children in the Middle Grades.*[4]

---

[3] U.S. Department of Health, Education and Welfare. OE-35068. Write to ERIC. National Cash Register Co. 4936 Fairmount Ave. Bethesda, Maryland 20014. Order No. ED 010 331.

[4] U.S. Government Printing Office, Washington, D.C. 1965. Catalogue No. FS 5.235:35068. Price 25c.

chapter 6

Increasing the Holding Power of the High School

By the time a student has reached the ninth or tenth grade, the capacity of the school to alter his attitude has waned. Skills may be improved at any period in life, but a child's self-concept and assumptions of possibility are no longer malleable after he reaches high school. This does not mean he will never change, but that any transformation will be a process of maturity not under the control of the school. If slow learners are to benefit from high school, it is the school itself that must adapt.

In the past it has been very difficult for the school to adjust to the slow learner's requirements. It was much easier to blame the student for his own failure, since this only involved a small minority. The cost to society of that minority has now become prohibitive. Educators are aware of the problem but are reluctant to face up to its implications. To better illustrate the plight of the slow learner in the traditional high school, the following true episode is offered.

The Case of Jenny

In the eighth grade, Jenny exhibited a decidedly untidy appearance. Her dresses, obvious legacies from older siblings, hung on her like a winter wash line. Straggling hair framed a sad face with large features. The sores on her legs usually held a scab or two. Yet, after several weeks of school, the teacher had formed an attachment for Jenny. She possessed a dogged, pathetic ambition to better herself.

Mr. Jones found Jenny's intelligence quotient listed in her permanent record as 85. He viewed this with some skepticism since recorded IQ's from elementary schools are about as reliable an index of a child's intelligence as their shoe size, but in Jenny's case corroborating evidence was soon produced. Her hand writing was defiantly independent of the lines on the paper, while her spelling bore a startling resemblance to the original manuscript of "Beowulf."

All through the winter, Mr. Jones labored with Jenny, but when spring came there was little to show. Not having the heart to fail anyone who struggled so valiantly to produce sentence fragments without capitals, he passed her with a D.

How she negotiated the ninth grade he never knew, but he suspected equally charitable teachers had been moved by her persistence.

During the year, he had been moved to guidance counselor; so it came about that at the start of the tenth grade, a more mature but scarcely more attractive Jenny was seated in his office to be scheduled. He placed her in low sections, interviewed teachers to find the most understanding, and so began an epic struggle.

During her tenth grade, Mr. Jones changed some of Jenny's teachers twice; others he begged and cajoled to help her, but in spite of all efforts, Jenny failed English.

Jenny was crushed. "I couldn't understand *Great Expectations*," she wailed. "Those old-time words don't mean nothing to me. And I couldn't even remember ten lines of the *Odyssey*. I might as well quit now."

Mr. Jones shook his head. In the name of Heaven, he thought, why do we have to inflict those things on her? But he said firmly, "That's nonsense. You can go to summer school and make up the English. As an eleventh grader you will be eligible for our work-study program. We'll find you a job in the afternoon and you can attend school in the morning."

The work-study teacher found Jenny a job as a salesgirl in a chain store. Earning money did something miraculous to Jenny's self-respect. For the first time, she was successful at something. She began to dress better and to fix her hair. Reports from her employer were good.

Senior year came and the work-study program was repeated, but there the resemblence ended. There were only two senior English teachers, Scylla and Charybdis. Jenny's career foundered and sank between them. At the same time she failed U.S. Government, not having understood the workings of the Federal Reserve System.

"It's no use," Jenny conceded. "I've got a job and I'm going to quit. I could never pass two subjects in summer school. They don't want my anyway."

But the counselor was not about to quit. By this time it had become a personal vendetta between him and the system. "You're not quitting now," he said grimly. "You're going to summer school and be the first member of your family ever to get a high school diploma."

The next day Mr. Jones called his friend, the principal of the summer school. "I know how you feel, Bob," the principal said, "but what do you expect me to do?"

"Damn it! I expect you to 'temper the wind to the shorn lamb', like the Bible says."

When August came, Jenny's name was on the graduation list. On the day of the graduation it was sultry in the auditorium. No choral group sang. The school board member present to hand out diplomas was obviously anxious to finish. A sprinkling of relatives dotted the empty hall. Someone knocked an arm from a seat and it clattered loudly. But none of this dampened the glow on Jenny's face. Mr. Jones, watching from the back row, felt a trifle uneasy. He wondered if he had any right to interfere in another's life as he had done.

Today, if you visit the store where Jenny works, you will find her in charge of the tableware department. She dresses quite neatly and has her hair done every week.

The manager wishes he had more like her. She is married
to a post office employee. In their modest suburban home,
Jenny's diploma occupies a prominent spot.

Thank Heaven her husband and employer do not
know her intelligence quotient.

INTEGRATING THE PROGRAM
WITH THE MIDDLE SCHOOL

As emphasized in the preceding chapter, the slow learner needs a continuous program from K-12. If he has
received proper attention and support, he may arrive at the
ninth grade reading at the seventh grade level. This is
acceptable for high school and with some persistence he can
hope eventually to graduate. Unfortunately, all too many
enter high school reading at the fourth or fifth grade. No
standard curriculum can be stretched to accommodate this
lag. Text books might as well be written in Sanskrit as far as a
fourth grade reader is concerned.

Before adequate measures to meet the needs of slow
learners can be formulated, their exact status must be
determined. For this purpose, high school guidance counselors need to visit feeder schools and learn as much as
possible about rising ninth graders. If proper records have
been kept, pupil's school histories will be voluminous. It
should not be difficult to sit down with them and plan a
realistic high school program. Tailoring their schedules to
meet each individual's achievement, ability, and interests
should ensure a smooth entrance into high school.

IDENTIFYING STUDENTS WHO NEED HELP

Enrollment in high school is only the beginning. Those
students who have not adjusted well to middle school should
be studied carefully. Symptoms to alert counselors are be-

havior problems, poor attendance, and immaturity, as well as poor achievement. Moreover, growth in early adolescence proceeds in sudden spurts which can develop into serious problems almost overnight. Rapid growth also creates obsolesence in the validity of test scores from elementary and middle schools.

Many ninth graders will be received from schools not in the system. Their records are often meager. As soon as possible after the beginning of school, counselors should administer new tests for the purpose of reevaluation and particularly for the purpose of identifying slow learners with special needs. The most satisfactory tests for this are The School and College Ability Tests and the Sequential Tests of Educational Progress.[1] Their validation group includes almost the entire national school population, lending them unusual reliability. A word of caution still needs to be added. It is quite doubtful if they are culturally fair to the disadvantaged. Great care needs to be taken to ensure answers are not marked at random, as often happens in large groups. In the case of slow learners and the disadvantaged, some reward needs to be offered for careful compliance with all provisions of testing. A score that is incorrect is worse than none at all.

COUNSELING FOR SELF-UNDERSTANDING

Individual counseling is a necessity for slow learner ninth graders, but must procede slowly. Their hostility to school, their aversion to study, their animosity toward teachers, and their general nihilism, require great patience and empathy. Adding to the counselor's difficulty is their stubborn unrealism about their goals, often derived from par-

---

[1] From Educational Testing Service. Princeton, N.J.

ent's lack of insight regarding their own children or the educational requirements for employment. Children new to the school are understandably reticent and suspicious. They are reluctant to talk to strange adults. All of this requires many counseling sessions. Rather than sit and wait for them to talk, as some counselors advocate, it is better to question them about themselves and their likes and dislikes. Let them voice their grievances without show of disapproval and you will at least have your foot in the door. Demonstrate friendly interest in their school experience and their future. If possible, do a concrete act of helpfulness. This could be replacing a lost book, obtaining a job or work permit, providing tutorial assistance, introducing them to the coach, changing their schedules, interceding with the principal or securing an appointment to an SCA committee.

Those who have been assigned to a special program such as the school-within-a-school are apt to be resentful and sensitive to any devaluation. One of the best means of countering this feeling is to rely on older students who have been successful in the same program. In the case of minority students, one or more of their race must always explain the proposal and its benefits to them. The U.S. Army, throughout its policy of educating recruits who fail the educational examination, uses the buddy system, paring a successful student with the slow learner. This is highly effective but difficult to work out in public schools.

However accomplished, slow learners must begin to trust the counselor before he can proceed with the important business of realistic goal setting. Above all, they need to understand and accept themselves without this increasing their insecurity. For this reason, the counselor needs to start with their strong points. Most will assert that they have none, but under persistent questioning will admit they do some things better than others. Show them how these qualities can be strengthened and built into assets.

WHAT TYPE OF CURRICULUM IS NEEDED?

No standard high school curriculum can be stretched to accommodate all academically-handicapped students. The genuine slow learner is working anywhere from the fourth through the seventh grade, the disadvantaged from the third through the sixth grade, while some emotionally-disturbed children may have very poor marks but nevertheless be reading as high as the eleventh grade.

Since we began with the premise that the school must change to suit the slow learner, special provisions must be made for them without prejudicing the education of the majority of the students. Simply grouping them into low sections while using the same text books and same teachers is no solution. Even worse is sending them to a special school, for this fastens upon them the stigma of inferiority. They need the same acceptance and chance for success as other students. With a few possible exceptions, they do *not* need higher mathematics or science, such as geometry or chemistry. They do *not* need English literature or rules of formal grammar. They do *not* need to do term papers or research. What they *do* need is to be able to read magazines and newspapers, to do fundamental mathematical calculations, to write legibly, and to punctuate simple sentences, to understand the structure of our society and their stake in it. Most of all, they need to learn a saleable skill that will enable them to find a suitable job and support a family.

FITTING THE CURRICULUM TO THE INDIVIDUAL

A necessary start is to know where each individual is. This information can be furnished by the guidance department, a topic already covered. Knowing the facts, however, is useless unless a strategy can be devised to fit the curriculum to the needs of each individual. Obviously, what we need is not *one* curriculum but one for each student. This is a slight exaggeration but fundamentally true, and calls for a new concept in teaching.

More flexibility in subject matter will be required as well as closer contact between student and teacher. Literally, the curriculum must be manufactured on the spot as needed. Fortunately, two innovations, currently holding the interest of educators, both meet the specifications. They are team teaching and the school-within-a-school. Such programs are being conducted in a number of systems. The author has served on two such teams and found the idea sound and feasible. Any program will experience difficulties initially, but its success will grow with experience.

THE SCHOOL-WITHIN-A-SCHOOL
AND TEAM TEACHING

The primary task is to select the proper team. Only volunteers should be accepted. They need not have impressive depth in their field but should be firm in their belief that teaching children is more important than teaching subject matter. They must cheerfully accept any assignment the team decides upon. Ability to work with colleagues, a good sense of humor, a willingness to experiment, and a tolerance for frustration are all important assets. The team should operate directly under the supervision of a sympathetic administrator, such as an assistant principal, who can represent them in policy-making circles and act as arbitrator in friendly disagreements.

Requirements of each situation will dictate the make-up of the team, but a typical group would comprise: a reading specialist, a counselor, one or more English and social studies teachers, a mathematics teacher, a science teacher, two vocational shop teachers, and a home economics teacher. These instructors would be assisted by three teacher's aides. This basic structure could be altered according to the formula: one teacher equals two teacher's aides or four secretaries. Such a team could handle 150 students at a ratio of 15 to 1. Where the number of students to be taught is larger, a second team should be formed. Adding teachers and students tends to make the structure unwieldy.

This team would assume responsibility for the education of 150 students, sometimes called a pod, except for physical education, typing, art and music. They would comprise a school-within-a-school, deciding what is to be taught each student, how it is to be taught, and what grades each student is to receive. They would take charge of the pod in the ninth grade and follow it through the tenth. Although they cannot be expected to have full authority for discipline, they would handle all minor infractions, absences, and tardies. After an initial summer in-service preparation, the team would be self-perpetuating, training its own replacements. The eleventh and twelfth grade English, U.S. History, and U.S. Government teachers would assume responsibility for the same students, although no longer as a pod, beginning with the eleventh grade. These teachers should be trained by the team, so that a continuity of program is maintained.

The school-within-a-school is designed to permit slow learners to mingle with the student body at the same time that they are receiving special teaching. All of them would take physical education with other students as well as those electing art, music, or typing. Classrooms and lockers would not be in a separate part of the building, but arranged so that slow learners would mix with others in the halls and cafeteria.

Schedules would be flexible, varying from week to week. Drills should always be conducted during the first two periods of the day and never for more than 30 minutes per subject. No class period should exceed 40 minutes, except for science or films. As much small group work and individual tutoring as possible should be scheduled. For tutoring and for out-of-school study, upperclassmen preparing to be teachers can be enlisted.

The school-within-a-school should be equipped with latest audio-visual devices, as well as teaching machines in carrels and directional readers. Most drill will be conducted with these devices and followed by some privilege such as a recreational period which can be withdrawn in case an individual does not attempt a satisfactory performance.

Planning should be done at a team conference each day while experiences are fresh in the instructor's mind. If this cannot be arranged during the regular school day, team members should be paid for an extra hour past contract time.

Vocational classes should be kept as practical as possible. This makes school meaningful to slow learners and simultaneously enables them to explore vocational choices which should be firm by the eleventh grade. Areas to be covered in shop are: auto mechanics, building trade clusters, sheet metal work, foundry and machine shop clusters, as well as pre-technical training in drafting and electricity. The home economics teacher will instruct girls in such pre-vocational skills as: food and clothing services, child care, housing, and institutional craft, in addition to home making tasks. Girls electing typing would not participate in this class.

Upon reaching the eleventh grade, students in the pod would elect either vocational training, business education, or work-study programs under the Distributive Education or Industrial Cooperative Training teachers. The only academic classes required would be English III and IV, U.S. History, and U.S. Government. Teachers of these subjects would be team-trained to ensure sympathetic progress of the student toward graduation.

After a few months together, a group solidarity develops between the students themselves and between the students and teachers which is very beneficial to learning. If teachers accompany students on field trips, join them in games, have picnics and dances together, the pod, in some respects, takes on the characteristics of a large family, sharing experiences and helping each other. This alters the slow learner's attitude toward teachers radically. Students draw support from the group as a whole and begin to feel more identity with the school. One great advantage is the ability to involve slow learners in extra-curricular activities. They can form their own clubs, put on their own shows and assemblies, and publish their own newspaper.

The teaching team itself begins to know each child personally and assumes responsibility for his learning. Over a period of time they develop methods of teaching and evolve various strategies that constitute a valuable accumulation of knowledge for aiding academic cripples.

Some problems can be anticipated initially. A few pupils will be hostile, feeling that they have been classified as retarded, but after a year of operation, satisfied and successful pod members will be your best salesmen.

Depending on the location, some difficulty will be encountered in maintaining a balance of races and sexes. At all cost, the pod must not be overloaded with minority students, nor with a preponderance of boys. The best guide to follow is to achieve a fair representation of the student body.

Objection from some parents must also be anticipated. It is best to explain the project to them before school starts and to invite them to come in and see it in action. A party or tea prepared by the students themselves, to which parents are invited, generates good will. Invitations to accompany their children on field trips should be mailed occasionally to parents. The more parents are involved in the project, the greater will be the expectations for success. However, no student should feel forced into the pod. Those who insist on being separated must be returned to regular classes. After a few successful years, the above difficulties will disappear.

The major problem is to make lessons meaningful to students who have acquired a dislike for school. Teachers in these teams can contribute significantly to educational knowledge by devising new methods of instruction to help students who may never learn to read satisfactorily still gain vital knowledge and skills. Some methods which hold promise are:

1. Extensive use of films visual aides, tapes, and records.
2. Group discussion.
3. Combined oral, visual, and tactile instructions to reinforce each other.
4. Models, games, simulations, mock-ups.
5. Demonstrations.
6. Role playing.
7. Involvement in experiments.

As in all education, *the teacher is the lesson.* Nothing can surpass a combination of friendliness, understanding, firmness, and realism. At Mt. Vernon High School in Fairfax County, Virginia, a program for students with learning difficulties has been in successful operation for a number of years. The academic instructor, Henry Sterle, undoubtedly one of the finest teachers of slow learners in the nation, has given permission to use the following suggestions:

1. All test papers should be graded by the students themselves.
2. All work done badly should be repeated or corrected by the student himself.
3. All test questions should be written out on the test paper with the answers underneath.
4. All directions pertaining to work should be written out on the chalk board and discussed.
5. All papers turned in must be uniform as to name, date, subject and question number. This teaches orderliness. Stress the importance of following directions.
6. Papers, books and instructional materials, checked out

from the teacher, must be replaced in the proper order. A clean, neat environment will grow on them. Get them to help you straighten up the class room, close windows, wash the chalk board.

7. Praise and encourage them whenever possible.
8. Movies should always be discussed prior to and immediately after being shown.
9. In writing letters or sample paragraphs, let them copy examples for the first few times.
10. Have the better students help the poorer ones on repeated or corrected work.
11. Make certain all back work is made up during class time.
12. Grade on attitude and progress (work completed).
13. Keep classroom atmosphere pleasant, relaxed, and informal, but disciplined.
14. When they work well, suggest they can stop 10 minutes before the end of the period.
15. Take an interest in their families, out-of-school hobbies, or shop projects. When they have employment in the evening, go visit them on the job.
16. Find opportunities to do small favors for them.
17. Stress the importance of their establishing good credit in society.
18. Always explain why you forbid them to do anything.
19. Teach and show by example, the important things they may not have learned at home, such as: manners, fair play, consideration of others, and orderliness.
20. Sometimes, put a mistake on the board. This gets their attention and builds their egos when they discover it.
21. Instruction in math should be kept simple, presented in basic steps, demonstrated and repeated several times. Label exercises so they have practical meaning to them such as: highway math, retail store math, banking and borrowing math, salesman's math, payroll math, baseball math, racing math, etc.

To paint too sanguine a picture for the school-within-a-school would be misleading. Nowhere in this volume does the author intend to imply that all students will be reached or helped by any suggestion. There are some students so restless they are unable to adjust to society's requirements in or out of school. Reaching them must wait for further discoveries into the causes of human behavior. Nevertheless, the school-within-a-school is a great advance over traditional high school methods.

WORK-STUDY PROGRAMS

Slow learners from the school-within-a-school program who do not choose vocational or business training in the eleventh grade should be placed in a work-study program. The most widely used in schools are Distributive Education and Industrial Cooperative Training, both established and partially supported by the federal government. They permit a student to attend school for a half-day to complete his academic requirements for a diploma, but for the balance of the day to work at a job. These students have one class period a day which teaches them such vocational skills as salesmanship, how to apply for a job, how to use the cash register, how to get along with fellow employees, how to meet the employer's requirements. They receive one school credit for this class. On the job, they are paid regular wages and receive a second school credit. The work-study teacher supervises them on the job, as well as in the class room, while their employer also grades their work. Even vocational and business training students are able to participate in work-study in their senior year. This facilitates their transition from school to employment.

These programs have been highly successful in reducing dropouts in the last two years of high school for a number of reasons.

1. They give the slow learner an opportunity to escape his school image of failure and prove himself in a new situation.
2. Employment is meaningful to slow learners. Earning money and performing a useful service competently builds self-respect and strengthens egos.

3. Acquaintance with the hard reality of business gives them a new perspective on the value of education.
4. When they do graduate from high school, they are equipped with work experience which is very valuable in finding a permanent job. Many stay on the job full time with the same company. Opportunities for advancement are enhanced where the employer has management training or finances further education and training.
5. D.E. and I.C.T. programs have their own clubs, teams, contests, and dances. For the first time, slow learners begin to participate in extra-curricular activities, all of which increases their identification with school and education.
6. I.C.T. students often receive what amounts to apprenticeship training in such subjects as landscape gardening, cosmetology, dental assistant and x-ray technician.

One of the major drawbacks to work-study programs is the custom, in many schools, of scheduling participants into regular classrooms. This means that they are once again in competition with superior students and are viewed with distaste by English teachers who insist they read Chaucer. For this reason, English and social studies teachers who are to handle work-study pupils should be specially picked.

A MEANINGFUL VOCATIONAL TRAINING AND PLACEMENT PROGRAM

Proof of the excellence of any vocational training program is in placement. If graduates of the program cannot find a job, their training is a fraud. Too often, the courses offered are not geared to local industrial demand or do not represent the level of skill necessary to perform the work required by employers. Schools must make greater efforts to hire skilled instructors regardless of certification requirements. When teachers are not skilled craftsmen, the courses become merely surveys that are textbook oriented. Many schools have antiquated equipment. If the graduate succeeds in finding a job, he is unacquainted with the tools and machinery in current use.

All of these deficiencies will quickly surface and hopefully be corrected if the school operates its own placement service. Guidance personnel have been trained for this task, which is a logical extension of their responsibilities. Graduates placed in suitable positions become the program's best salesmen. Counselors often experience difficulties in persuading slow learners to take vocational courses because of their blue collar status, yet skilled training represents the best and most realistic choice for slow learners to be absorbed into society. A much better job of promoting vocational training to students and particularly to parents can be done if satisfied and successful graduates can be used for reference or brought back to the school to speak.

Vocational programs should not be made dumping grounds for all behavior problems other teachers do not want. Such problems can better be handled in work-study programs. Nor should vocational programs become de facto segregated by disadvantaged students who need academic education. Vocational training should be business-like and thorough. Students not willing to abide by such rules should be removed. Being half-trained is worthless to them and results in bad publicity for the program among employers.

On the other hand, there is a tendency for vocational teachers to raise standards so high the slow learner is frozen out. Administrators need to resist this and insure that any student willing to apply himself realistically to learning a trade will have that opportunity.

MOTIVATING THE HARD-CORE

Teachers who actually instruct the hard-core are often cynical when they read or hear rosy accounts of techniques and class room practices that seem to promise wonders in motivating potential dropouts. These teachers do not disparage the many fine experiments being conducted, but they have tried most of them and know that in the light of cold, harsh reality some students are unreachable by any known means. These students have a cynical antagonism for schools and school personnel. Their habitual attitude toward society is a personal vendetta with all forms of restriction. Evading controls provides them with the "kicks" they seek to assure themselves they are actually discrete individuals, possessing the ability to control their own lives. The deep-seated cause of this reaction is a punitive sense of worthlessness which they attempt to suppress. Since they cannot succeed in hiding from themselves their true status, they engage in a running battle with authority which clouds and partially obscures reality, both for themselves and those in contact with them. Knowing the cause of their behavior is of little value to teachers and counselors, since schools possess no weapon powerful enough to deal with such attitudes.

Although it may outrage the ethical standards of middle class educators to stoop to a form of bribery, they must either concede defeat or themselves face up to reality and use whatever methods are necessary and available to keep unreachable students in classrooms.

The hard-core student is shrewd enough not to turn down a "good thing," so it is possible to offer him a meaningful reward for stipulated performance. Some suggestions that have been tried are:

1. A coke break, contigent upon satisfactory completion of an assignment.
2. Use of the community or school swimming pool.
3. A field trip to a movie or sporting event.
4. Privileges of a smoking or recreation room.
5. Points which can be accumulated and then cashed for tickets to movie houses or skating rinks.

Such artificial stimulation cannot be continued indefinitely, but any extra time the hard-core dropout can be kept off the streets is worthwhile. Hopefully, some will find they are learning and no longer need to be bribed—others will have time to grow up and realize where their best interests lie.

HELPING THEM IDENTIFY WITH THE SCHOOL WITH SUITABLE EXTRA-CURRICULAR ACTIVITIES

In most high schools, extra-curricular activities are a privileged reservation monopolized by the successful students. Good grades are required for participation in many activities, such as service clubs, honor societies and student government. Work-study students are automatically barred from athletic teams and other after-school activities because they work in the afternoons. Whether other arrangements could be made is debatable, but there is no defense for the fact that the students who do take part in school affairs form an unofficial establishment which mutually supports its own members and governs the social life of the student body, both in and out of school. When a human relations council was recently established in the author's school, where morale had always been considered high, both faculty and students were shocked by the bitter voices of lower class students and slow learners who felt frozen out of the school's social life. The rising voice of the underprivileged is rocking the nation, and no more appropriate place to understand its grievances exists than in the public schools. Channels of communication need to be opened in every school between students and faculty. But more needs to be done. School social life needs a drastic overhaul to invite participation by those students not well-off or academically talented.

School buildings should be thrown open nights and

week-ends to social activities that do not require expensive clothes or costly visits to beauty salons. If any teacher or administrator doubts the above statement, he can check for himself at the next school dance. Count the number of underprivileged attending. When the drill team performs at the next football game, observe how many lower class girls are in the line-up.

This does not require that administrators go to the opposite extreme and turn schools over to everyone who protests. Good order and the right to walk unmolested in the halls is essential to good learning, but ways can be found to include all in the school's social life. Most underprivileged want only to be brought into the group, not destroy it.

HOW COUNSELORS CAN WORK WITH THE HOME AND TEACHERS

Communication with students, particularly with the disadvantaged and emotionally disturbed, is more essential now than ever before. Today's youth are remarkably idealistic and innocent, seeking almost to court disaster by scorning reality. Their poetry, painting, and music reflect a quality of fantasy that deliberately avoids meaning. When the consequences of their behavior does take a serious turn, they either greet it with a resigned fatalism or appear resentful and put-upon. Self-blame simply does not seem to exist for them. They blithely ignore and even deny the serious effects of drugs, tobacco, and alcohol. For those with poor control, weak egos and negative self-images, the consequences of this illusion often prove tragic. The youth who repeatedly has his license suspended for speeding or drunk driving is soon involved in a fatal accident. The young car thief on parole is soon guilty of recidivism. The young, unwed mother, helped through her ordeal, soon embraces drugs and prostitution.

The hard-core deliquent does not want to communicate. He simply wants his own way. Counselors who sincerely wish to help them must resist the temptation to condone self-destructive behavior. Reality is the counselor's only prescription. Students who can be made to see reality may be able to solve their own problems. Otherwise, they are pitiful masochists, bloodying their heads against the ultimate wall of consequences.

Listening to them non-judgmentally is very important. In many cases, no one has ever listened without censure before, but therapy does not end there. Lecturing or moralizing is futile. They simply tune you out, but their mistakes must be brought to light in a sincere, friendly manner. They must understand that you wish to help, but the only real help you can give is to assist them to understand what they are doing wrong—not morally wrong but practically wrong. It is never easy, and you may lose them, but if you do not try you cannot claim to be a professional.

Teachers and counselors both must understand the student's specific classroom problems and provide concrete help. If the student will accept tutorial assistance, the counselor must make the arrangements. The teacher should provide assistance in the form of expert advice, give instructions to the tutor and follow-up the results in the classroom.

Just as the teacher and counselor must work together, so must parent and counselor collaborate. This is vastly more difficult due to the emotional aura that surrounds the power structure of the family. Any disagreement which involves vested authority almost immediately escalates into bitter recriminations on the part of both parent and child, making communication impossible. Any attempt on the part of the counselor to reconcile differences usually fails.

An experiment was recently tried in the author's school which seems to hold some promise. Curiously enough, the suggestion came from students themselves. The class arranged a party with refreshments in the school cafeteria on a Sunday afternoon and invited their parents. After refreshments, two circles of 15 chairs each were arranged. The groups were seated with students and parents alternating, but students were not seated in the same circle with their parents. Two students had been appointed chairmen to lead the discussions. The agenda chosen covered such topics as homework, deadlines for being home at night, smoking, drinking, household chores, telephone usage, and selection of friends. Parents were, at first, on the defensive, but soon rallied and good naturedly took up the challenge. No agreements were attempted, but there was a remarkable absence of hostility on both sides and a willingness to see each other's view point. Both parents and students felt they had benefited from the exchange. One significant spin-off was noted in the classroom, following the discussion. Many students who formerly had been critical of their parents showed greater understanding for parental responsibilities.

Such a meeting must be carefully prepared so that parents are aware of what they are letting themselves in for, but in this case almost everyone was pleased and intrigued with the results. An open and frank exchange between the generations is preferable to the confrontation that often divides families into uncompromising enemy camps.

THE SUMMER INSTITUTE

Most school systems have operated summer schools for many years. When a student needs an extra subject to round out his program, to meet college requirements, or to strengthen his knowledge of algebra or French before proceeding to the next higher level, summer schools serve a legitimate purpose. In the past, however, summer schools have been packed with slow learners who have failed English or social studies in regular school. These students enter summer school several grades below the level they have just failed, but the same textbook they could not read and the same course content they could not understand was repeated, this time at an accelerated pace. By what reasoning they were expected to master in six weeks what they could not learn in nine months remained a mystery. Most students recognized it as a farce and gave up. For the teacher it became a long, hot summer. Not even Pestalozzi could have challenged them. The teacher usually extricated himself from the dilemma by passing those who tried hardest. If he passed too many he was not rehired for the next summer. Those who failed usually dropped out of school. In recent years, this ritual has been replaced by another, almost as ridiculous. Now all students who attend regularly are passed although the content of the course has still changed little. The reasoning now appears to be, the student who fails should be punished by attending school six weeks longer than other students. Recognizing its own contribution to his failure, the school does penance by passing him if he accepts his punishment. Neither procedure recognizes or grapples with the slow learner's real problems.

Beginning with the summer of 1967, many school systems adopted a new type of program, called the Summer Institute, funded in most cases by federal money. The institute usually consists of a team of five or six carefully screened teachers and counselors who are free to conduct the kind of program they feel would be meaningful for slow learners and particularly for disadvantaged children. Such a team, planning their program from day to day as they experiment with various techniques, can handle about 100 students. The possibilities for this type of program are enormous. There is still a tendency on the part of administrators and those who fund the programs to select too many major goals, causing the team to dissipate its energies in all directions, but the results far exceed those of the traditional summer school.

Since these teachers are experienced with and understand the needs of slow learners, they interest themselves in each student's welfare, getting to know them as individuals. Students are soon aware of this and a rapport develops between pupils and teachers similar to that of a large family. Everyone takes part in shows, in field trips, dances, and picnics. Group discussions are open forums where all share opinions equally. The gap between teacher and pupil vanishes. Lessons are taught on any level the teacher finds practical, and materials are selected from any source that appears to fit the needs. Students take part in planning much of the program, but teachers shape plans to meet their selected objectives. Grading is informal, based largely on the student's participation. Conferences are held regularly with counselors to keep students aware of their progress and to make future plans for the coming winter school session. Young college students or Youth Corps Workers are often employed as aides.

An illustration of how the institute can make its contribution can be perceived from the following example. Let us select one objective: "To provide eighty low-income, disadvantaged children age 12 to 15 with a variety of cultural experiences, calculated to raise their self-concept." Highlights of this program could include such events as:

1. *A Trip to a Historical Museum*—Not too much should be attempted at one time. Portions of the museum to be visited should be selected in advance and visited by the staff, who would then write stories of imaginary people using the items on display. These would be recorded on tape and played to the children in advance of the visit. Discussion would follow to familiarize students with what they would see. After the trip, students themselves could write and role play scenes in which these items would be involved.

2. *A Trip to a Good Restaurant*—Members of the staff would collect menus of several restaurants in advance. The children

would be acquainted with the kinds of dishes listed and prices of each. They would then decide where they wished to go and what they would like to order. Discussions would follow as to how to dress, how to use tableware and napkins, how to act in public, how to order and tip waiters.

3. *A Visit to a Concert*—Copies of the program to be performed would be obtained in advance and records of these selections purchased to be played in the classroom. The different instruments and the type of music to be played would be discussed.

4. *A Picnic at a Public Park*—A committee of students would visit a number of sites and select the one they found the most desirable. The students themselves would plan the menu. Groups of pupils would be sent to several supermarkets to compare prices on items selected. A budget would be adopted and small groups sent out to buy the food and accessories.

The above are merely suggestions. The ingenuity of the staff can be counted on to devise many more, such as a visit to an airport, a factory assembling autos, or a city legislative body. Planning and conducting these events themselves not only makes the trip more meaningful to students, but helps to raise their self-concept. They see themselves as individuals capable of holding a place in society.

SAMPLE PROGRAMS

The following is a course outline of a dropout project, previously referred to, now in its seventh year at Mt. Vernon High School, Fairfax County, Virginia. Research on this project was the basis for an article published by the author in *The School Counselor*.[2] Statistically significant gains in raising school achievement and reducing dropout rates were recorded.

Briefly, 30 boys, 15 in the ninth grade and 15 in the

---

[2] Shelton, Baker O. "Assigning a New Role to the Potential Drop Out." *The School Counselor.* Vol 13 No. 3 March 1966 p 182.

tenth grade, are kept together (except for physical education) both years, and for science (BSCS-SM in the tenth grade only). They are taught by two instructors, one who teaches English, mathematics, and geography (ninth grade only); the second teaches the shop course. These students are selected on the basis of three categories: (1) Those with personality, home, or emotional problems; (2) Those from low income brackets; (3) Those who lack native ability to master the requirements for high school graduation. Counselors select the participants and work closely with the program. Beginning with the eleventh grade, these students are fed into the county vocational program or into Mt. Vernon's work-study programs (Distributive Education and Industrial Cooperative Training). The dropout rate over the years stands at about 1%. A few students have enrolled in the local community college.

Main Objective

To graduate all students from high school with the academic knowledge and vocational skills consistent with their ability and a definite plan for the next step in their future.

Specific Objectives

1. To help each student to know and accept his strengths and weaknesses.

2. To help each student understand the obligations of good citizenship in a democracy.

3. To help each student see the world realistically and plan for the future sensibly.

4. To help each student understand his family and community obligations.

5. To help each student to understand his obligations to his employer.

6. To inform each student of his military obligations.

7. To teach each student the basic knowledge of budgeting, installment buying, and social security.

8. To teach each student how to look for employment, how to conduct himself during an interview, and how to fill out an application.

9. To acquaint each student with the educational and vocational opportunities open to him and with the necessity of staying in school as long as possible.

Main Objectives of the Academic Program

1. To help each student understand the fundamentals of basic mathematical computation.

2. To raise each student's reading level as high as possible.

3. To teach each student to write legibly and speak coherently.

4. To teach each student to spell the basic words and write a simple sentence.

Methods (Academic Program)[3]

"A stated objective of this program is to provide a high degree of flexibility in instruction toward meeting the special needs of the vocational education student.

"As a general rule, no homework is required. Work done outside of class is a product of individual initiative. Text books are not issued as a prime source of material, but are employed from time to time in class, as the situation dictates, as supplementary material. All completed work is corrected and discussed. No letter or numerical grade is assigned, however. The lecture method of instruction is minimized. New material is discussed briefly before starting work. As students work in class to complete an assigned lesson, individual instruction pertaining to the work at hand is effected. Notwithstanding film scheduling a year in advance, the supplementary film program is necessarily keyed to availability. A heavy film program is utilized because of the high interest and motivational levels achieved by this medium. All films are discussed before and after viewing to highlight key features and to stress vocational correlations."

---

[3] Reprinted with permission of Henry Sterle, Homer C. Currence, instructors, and Stewart Christiano, assistant principal for instruction and Melvin Landes, principal.

COURSE OUTLINE 1968–1969
VOCATIONAL SPECIAL EDUCATION—GRADE 9

	ENGLISH	MATHEMATICS	GEOGRAPHY
First Nine Weeks	*Usage*—Spelling, Pronouns, Vocabulary, Tense, etc. *Use of Dictionary* *Writing Paragraphs*—Structure	*Whole Numbers*— Basic Operations *Measurement*—Board Feet, Shop Measurements	*Finding Out About the Earth*—Before the age of discovery—from the age of discovery on *Current Affairs* *Maps and Charts*
Second Nine Weeks	*Usage*—Spelling, Pronouns. Vocabulary, Tense, etc.—Rules of Capitalization *Postal and Banking Information* *The Business Letter*	*Fractional Numbers*—Basic Operations *Measurement*— Linear *Graphs*—Broken-Line, Bar & Circle Graphs	*Cultural Areas of the World*—Man on the Land, European Culture Area, American Culture Area *Current Affairs* *Maps and Charts*
Third Nine Weeks	*Usage*—Spelling, Pronouns, Vocabulary, Tense, etc. *Telephone Conversations* *Classified Ads* *Business Conversation*	*Decimal Fractions*—Basic Operations *Measurement*—Two Dimensional, Three Dimensional	No. African—S.W. Asian Culture Area Oriental Culture Area Soviet Culture Area African Culture Area *Current Affairs* *Maps and Charts*
Fourth Nine Weeks	*Usage*—Spelling, Pronouns, Vocabulary, Tense, etc. *Interviews* *Attitudes Toward Supervisors and Co-Workers*	*Percentages*— Interest, Taxes, Commission, Discount *Managing Your Money*—Installment Buying, Insurance	*Pacific Culture Area* *Geography and You*—Using man's knowledge of the land. *Current Affairs* *Maps and Charts*

COURSE OUTLINE 1968–1969
VOCATIONAL SPECIAL EDUCATION—GRADE 10

	ENGLISH	MATHEMATICS
First Nine Weeks	Usage—Spelling, Pronouns, Vocabulary, Tense, etc. Writing Paragraphs—Structure Business Conversation	Whole Numbers—Basic Operations Measurements—Board Feet, Shop Measurements Graphs
Second Nine Weeks	Usage—Spelling, Pronouns, Vocabulary, Tense, etc. Composition Reference Books Postal and Banking Information	Fractional Numbers—Basic Operations Measurement—Linear Personal Finances—Installment Buying, Insurance
Third Nine Weeks	Usage—Spelling, Pronouns, Vocabulary, Tense, etc. Composition Telephone Conversations Telegrams & Memorandums The Business Letter	Decimal Fractions—Basic Operations Measurement—Two dimensional, Three dimensional Basic Math. in Electricity
Fourth Nine Weeks	Usage—Spelling, Pronouns, Vocabulary, Tense, etc. Composition Classified Ads Employment Procedures	Percentages—Interest, Taxes, Commission, Discount Basic Math. in Navigation, Gunnery and Aviation

English

"*Usage* (vocabulary, spelling, tenses, pronouns, etc.)—The basic unit of work, the lesson, usually consists of a prepared, mimeographed handout which is worked in class over a period of two to three days. Utilitarian and business-oriented usage is stressed. Periodic written assignments are evaluated partially on effective usage and spelling. Use of the dictionary is stressed heavily. Crossword puzzles from *Scope Magazine,* the local newspapers, and other sources are employed."

"*Reading*—Reading materials are chosen largely by the students on the basis of group and individual maturity and reading ability. Most materials have a direct or indirect vocational correlation. Paper backs and periodicals make up the bulk of reading materials. *Scope Magazine* is a regular reading source. In response to the irregular study and work habits of these students, approved reading is always available as a constructive alternative to work at hand. Taken together, the reading and composition complete the read, comprehend, and express sequence of the language arts program."

Mathematics

"As in English, the basic lesson is generally a prepared mimeograph handout which is worked in class over a two to three day period. Basic computational skills are stressed throughout the program. Special emphasis is placed upon practical, 'real-life' problem solving of a business, commercial, or personal nature."

Objectives of the Shop Program

1. To teach the basic skills, knowledges, understandings, and habits that are common to numerous types of industrial occupations.

2. To teach the basics that might help the individual to find himself and advance to more specific training.

3. To teach the individual to be prepared to obtain and hold some type of employment by developing desirable work habits, attitudes, and abilities to get along with others.

chapter 7

Teaching English to the Slow Learner

Before beginning this chapter, it would be pertinent to inquire into the purpose for teaching English to slow learners. What use will they make of the knowledge and skills learned in an English class? Is familiarity with formal grammar a requisite? Will literary appreciation be important in their lives? Such tasks have proven very difficult for them in the past. Many have been taught grammar for years, yet know little or nothing about it. Surely this time could have been spent more profitably.

Common sense dictates that slow learners will use English mainly for communication. Meaning, not form or style, will have paramount importance to them. Their conversation will be standard English, necessary to secure employment and manage their daily lives. Their reading matter will consist of newspapers, magazines and paperback books. Their listening will be confined to radio, television, and motion pictures. Their writing will be limited to simple notes and letters. This much knowledge of English they will need and this much they can learn. Teaching, however, must be kept simple, practical and thorough. Such skills as spelling and vocabulary usage should be overlearned through a variety of ingenious, spaced drills, including tapes. Handwriting, long neglected, should be practiced until legible. Plastic letteroverlays are effective in correcting letter formation and slant. Transparencies, now on the market, enlarge the letters to emphasize the correct pattern. Most slow learners have a well-developed kinesthetic sense that can be utilized in teaching handwriting by tracing, as in the Fernald Method.

Children with no physiological handicaps learn instinctively to communicate in whatever language is used by the adults surrounding them, although recent discoveries by Dr. Noam Chomsky seem to reveal a universal grammar in the speech of young children, regardless of the language. Irrespective of how they learn, children do a remarkably competent job of teaching themselves to speak, within the limits of their environment. Yet, their natural abilities are sufficient only to permit them to speak and listen. Left to themselves, they would never learn to read and write. School, then, is the interface between verbal and written communication, and this is where the trouble begins. The reason so many children encounter difficulty in associating the written word with the spoken word is still a mystery to reading specialists. No positive method of teaching reading, applicable to all children, is known. There are, however, certain clues to guide the English teacher.

1. There is an optimum time to teach reading, varying with each child. If this time is missed, reading troubles accumulate.
2. Instruction must pursue maturity. First, children learn to speak, next they learn to read, then they learn to write.
3. In reading, a child utilizes his reservoir of knowledge. He can only communicate with the writer if both have shared actual or learned experiences.
4. Children learn to react to a greater number of words by ear than by sight. Relation of the spoken to the written word is essential in reading instruction.

5. Poor readers interpret symbols to be specific objects instead of classes of objects. Symbols should, therefore be avoided until considerable facility in reading is attained.
6. Perception can be aided by use of all the senses—hearing, touch, taste, smell and sight.

TEACHING SLOW LEARNERS TO READ
THE WAY A CHILD LEARNS

Slow learners read at many levels and an attempt to diagnose their placement can be made by using the Gates-MacGinite Reading Tests[1] for grades K-12. For non-readers their usefulness is doubtful. A student who cannot read cannot take the test. In such a case, the only way to start is to assume that he knows nothing. Where reading machines with tapes and complete systems are available, such as EDL Controlled Reading Sets, Language 100 or Study-Skills Mini Systems,[2] much preparation time can be saved, but the teacher, not so fortunate, can still prepare her own program, using only a tape recorder and an overhead projector.

Step #1—Determine your student's basic vocabulary by having them talk into the tape recorder. Have them relate stories or incidents such as: "This Happened to Me on the Way to School," "The Last Time I Was Sick," "The Game I Like Most to Play." Also, show them photographs taken near the school and ask them what they see. Urge them to describe and name specific objects and people. Get them to use action words.

When these tapes are transcribed, a basic oral vocabulary emerges. It may vary from 300 words at the first grade to 1500 at the ninth grade. Since they can use these words orally, presumably they can learn to recognize them visually.

[1] Teachers College Press. Teachers College, Columbia University 525 West 120th St, New York, N.Y. 10027.
[2] Educational Developmental Laboratories Inc. Huntington, New Jersey.

Step #2—Descriptive or narrative paragraphs can be composed by the teacher using only words from the basic vocabulary. Choose a subject corresponding with the interests of the students, and deal only with their familiar environment. The teacher should then tape these items, speaking slowly and using correct standard English. As far as possible, structure should follow the student's own speech pattern and idiom, but the sentences should be simple, comprehensible, and grammatically correct. Play the tapes over a number of times until the students can recognize each word, then combine the tape with the overhead projector. Enlarge difficult words, drawing lines under the letters that form a syllable when the sound of that syllable is heard. Halt the tape to illustrate vowel and consonant sounds on the screen. Demonstrate prefixes and suffixes in the same manner, giving particular attention to the pronounciation of endings. Interest in this drill can be maintained for only a short time during one showing, but do not move ahead until the students have acquired a verbal memory of each paragraph. Play the tapes over a number of times, having the class repeat the words with the tape. Let them use a second recorder and compare their own recordings with those of the teacher. Change the tapes often but adhere to the basic vocabulary words. Only when you are satisfied that the class can fairly accurately pronounce each basic vocabulary word are you ready for Step #3.

Step #3—Mimeograph your paragraphs and give each student a copy. Then, play the tape and have them read the printed word as the tape sounds the oral word. They may need to use a pencil to follow along under each line, pausing to identify each separate word as it is pronounced. It may be well to put the written paragraph on the overhead projector at the same time, using a pointer to identify each word as the tape speaks it. Continue this until the students can recognize on paper each word of their basic oral vocabulary. When they are able to read the paragraph correctly without the tape, you are ready to move on to Step #4.

Step #4—You must begin now to introduce new words. Secure any list of most commonly used words (for example)[3]. Select words used most frequently, not in the student's basic oral vocabulary. Proceed slowly, presenting only a few words at a time. Using the overhead projector, first establish the pronounciation, second, give the meaning in terms of your student's experience, illustrated (if possible) with a simple drawing. Then, compose a few sentences using the word in several contexts. When you feel that the student's comprehension is satisfactory, compose, tape, and mimeograph a new paragraph, using the basic vocabulary but introducing a few new words. Then, allow the students to hear and see it at the same time. This will be a slow process, but remember, they may have been exposed to reading for six or seven years before you knew them, yet have learned almost nothing. When you are satisfied that they have a substantial vocabulary of most commonly used words, you are ready for Step #5.

Step #5—Secure enough copies of a paperback book for each student. Select a suitable reading level but with appropriate interest and ethnic subject matter. Most publishers have lists to choose from. Several suggestions are: *"The Outsiders,"* written by a 17 year old boy;[4] *"I've Got a Name"*[5] and *"Trouble After School."* Go through a few pages and select unfamiliar words, introducing them as previously outlined. Tape about 15 minutes of the book and play the

---

[3] Thorndyke, E.L. and Lorge, I. *The Teacher's Word Book of 30,000 Words,* New York. Teachers College, Columbia University. Bureau of Publications. 1944.

[4] Dell Publishing Co., Inc. 750 Third Ave., New York, 10017. 1967.

[5] Holt, Rinehart and Winston, Inc. New York, N.Y.

[6] Scholastic Book Services. Scholastic Magazines. 904 Sylvan Ave., Englewood Cliffs, N.J. 07632.

tape to them. Then, replay it, having them read silently with the spoken word. This can be continued indefinitely, but after a few books, step #6 should be introduced.

Step #6—Secure 50 or 100 paperback books and display them in the classroom in the same fashion drug stores use. Allow students a free choice in selecting books to take home if they so desire. You will be missing a lot of books, but you will have them started reading for the first time in their lives.

OTHER ACTIVITIES IN READING
FOR MIDDLE AND HIGH SCHOOL

It will not be necessary to start all slow learners at the primitive level just described, but the process can be entered upon at almost any level. If the slow learner can read at the fifth, sixth, or seventh grade level, a number of remedial techniques now in use can be employed. A simple formula for estimating reading level without testing is to select a text book used in the grade being taught. Instruct the student to read orally. If he cannot recognize 95 out of every 100 words or give back 75% of paragraph comprehension, the book is too difficult for him.

One favored method for improving reading ability is to cultivate listening ability as a prelude. Listening and reading are similar processes, one using sound to acquire meaning, the other sight to acquire meaning. Tape material to be studied and play the tape to them. Follow this with oral questions. Then, have them read the same material and follow with written questions.

Do not insist on slow learners reading fast. Speed will never be essential to them, but meaning, which they acquire slowly, will be a necessity. Discuss material before and after reading. If it has been wisely selected, it will contain something of interest to them, and prior discussion will motivate them to read more.

A program to improve basic reading skills of slow learners in junior and senior high can be devised by the teacher, starting with (1) word recognition, (2) word meaning, (3) sentence meaning, and (4) paragraph meaning. A suggested outline would be similar to the following:

I. *Word attack by sound.*
   Vowel sounds, consonant sounds, syllables.
II. *Word attack by structure.*
   Prefixes, suffixes, compound words, root words.
III. *Word attack by context.*
IV. *Word attack by dictionary.*
V. *Comprehension.*
   Sentence meaning by key words, inference, sequence.
VI. *Comprehension.*
   Paragraph meaning, key sentences, choosing a title, understanding the main idea, acquiring the facts.

A number of work books with similar contents are on the market.[7] Better still, complete programs are available which supply individual cards for each student.[8]

READING MACHINES

There is much controversy among reading specialists as to the value of reading machines. It is certain that they are not panaceas, nor can they be relied on to do the job alone, but when employed correctly they have proved to be valuable teaching aids. There are a number of such machines on the market supplied with complete film strips and lessons.

[7] Basic Reading Skills for High School. Scott Foresman and Co. Chicago, Illinois.
[8] Tactics in Reading. Maintenance of Skills I. Scott Foresman & Co. SRA Reading Laboratories. Science Research Associates Inc., 259 East Erie St. Chicago, Illinois.

The most widely known are The Controlled Reader and The Tach-X. [9]

The Tach-X, a type of tachistoscope which flashes words on a screen at controlled intervals, is designed to aid word recognition, increase visual memory and improve spelling.

The Controlled Reader has a moving slot which unreels a line of words on the screen at any desired speed. It is designed to improve left to right reading ability, and reduce the time which the student has to recognize and associate a word with joining words.

The novelty of the machines appeals to slow learners. It focuses their attention, supplies individualized instruction, requires them to work in a systematic fashion, and helps to revive confidence in their ability to learn.

Many helpful ideas for teaching reading can be found in the *Journal of Reading*. [10] Other useful suggestions can be found in pamphlets from the New York City Board of Education. [11] A completely new and promising phonetic approach to reading instruction called "Distar" [12] uses programming to teach retarded readers in elementary school.

READING MATERIALS FOR SLOW LEARNERS

One of the most useful materials for teaching slow learners is the daily paper. In addition to carrying current news items that effect their lives directly, newspapers contain

---

[9] Supplied by Educational Development Laboratories, Inc., Huntington, N.Y.

[10] Published by the International Reading Association. Box 695 Newark, Delaware 19711.

[11] *Resource Units in Language Arts* for General Course Students in Senior High School. Board of Education. City of New York Publication Sales Office, 110 Livingston St., Brooklyn, N.Y. Price $1.50. Make check payable to Auditor, board of Education.

The Retarded Reader in Junior High School. Pamphlet #31 Price $1.00. Address same as above.

[12] Distributed by Science Research Associates, Inc. 259 East Erie St., Chicago, Illinois.

special interest sections appealing to students such as sports, cars, women's pages, comic pages, crossword puzzles, weather reports, etc. For the 11 to 15 age group who read at the second or third grade level, several weekly newspapers can be ordered.[13] Newspapers furnish an excellent opportunity to teach extracting the main idea in an article. Cut off the headlines and captions of short items and have the students write their own. Then, compare their captions with those of the newspaper.

Scholastic Scope[14] is one of the best magazines available for poor readers and disadvantaged students. They find it both readable and interesting. Other magazines which have many pictures and are intriguing to slow readers are: *Mechanix Illustrated, Sports Illustrated, Hot Rod* and *Life. Readers Digest* appeals to high school age readers, although the *Readers Digest* also publishes *Reading Skill Builders*[15] suitable for various grade levels.

For high school age non-readers, a programmed Reading Series of 21 books by Sullivan Associates[16] provides beginning readers an orderly introduction to the sounds, letters, and symbols of English.

Many publishers are reaching the market with books that have senior high school appeal but with fourth grade reading level.[17]

For older slow learners, a combination literature and composition book called *Voices in Literature, Language and Composition*[18] has a content and format suitable to lower achievement levels, but with teen age interest. It comes

[13] One such is published by American Education Publications, Education Center. Columbus, Ohio.
[14] Order from Scholastic Magazines, Inc. 902 Sylvan Ave., Englewood Cliffs, New Jersey.
[15] Readers Digest Association, Inc. Pleasantville, N.Y.
[16] Published by McGraw-Hill Book Company. 330 West 42nd St. New York, N.Y.
[17] Doubleday Signal Books. Doubleday & Co., Inc. Garden City, New York.
Scholastic Book Services. 904 Sylvan Ave. Englewood Cliffs, New Jersey.
[18] Ginn and Company. Statler Building. 125 Second Ave. Boston, Mass.

equipped with records, transparencies and work sheets which are useful to teachers.

For further sources of material, consult *English Journal,*[19] and *Media and Methods.*[20] Negro literature for secondary school students was listed in *English Journal,* May 1969.

Books the author has found which have almost universal appeal to slow learners are: *Hot Rod, Street Rod, The Red Car, Black Like Me, Catcher in the Rye, The Green Berets, Of Mice and Men, To Kill a Mockingbird, Thunderball, Goldfinger, The Time Machine.*

TEACHING COMPOSITION TO THE SLOW LEARNER

Style, modifiers, subordinate and parallel construction are of little use to slow learners. Their interest is in clarity, action, and details. Their writing will be confined to instructions, letters, and directions. For this purpose they need simple sentences using the noun-verb or noun-verb-noun construction. They do need to use basic punctuation, capitalization and spelling, which should be overlearned. Drill, using the overhead projector and teaching machines is probably the best method to use. Capitalization can be taught through the prime and shape technique or by programmed instruction often supplied by teaching machines.

Programmed instruction, although suited to slow learners, has not swept the schools as its advocates had hoped for several reasons:

1. Students have been conditioned to learn in groups, not as individuals. They need the stimulus of human contact.
2. After a period of time, programmed instruction becomes boring because of its inherent simplicity.

---

[19] Official Journal of Secondary Section, National Council of Teachers of English. 508 South 6th St., Champaign, Illinois.

[20] Media and Methods Institute, Inc. 134th N. 13th St. Philadelphia, Pennsylvania.

3. The reinforcement of discovering the correct answer immediately is theoretically sound, but it is not sufficiently rewarding to induce continuous application for more than a short period of time.
4. Most commercial programmed texts are suitable for good students, but many frames are too difficult for slow learners to grasp.

Any teacher can construct short programs to suit his own situation. An example to teach capitalization of proper nouns follows·

USING CAPITALS FOR PROPER NOUNS

Instructions

Read each frame—then write the word in the blank which *best* answers the directions. Check your answer at the bottom of the page before you go on to the next frame.

1.

ocean   One of these words is *one* special body of
Atlantic   water. Write the word here.

                                    *_____

2.

ocean   One of these words is *any* large body of
Atlantic   water. Write the word here.

                                    *_____

3.

house   One of these words is *one* special place to
White House   live. Write the word here.

                                    *_____

---

1. Atlantic 2. ocean 3. White House

4.

house   One of these words is *any* place to live.
White House   Write the word here.

*_____

5.

A word that names anything is called a
*_____

6.

tree   One of these words is a noun. Write the
killed   word here:
beautiful

*_____

7.

pencil   One of these words is *not* a noun. Write
push   the word here:
book

*_____

8.

Lincoln   A word that gives a name to a special
Chicago   person, place or thing is called a *proper* noun.
Apollo 12   The words at the right are
*_____ nouns.

9.

man   A word that gives a name to a group
city   (several things that are alike) of things is
capsule   called a *common* noun. The words at the left
are
*_____ nouns.

---

4. house 5. noun 6. tree 7. push 8. proper 9. common

10.

    nation   These nouns are

    women   *_____ nouns.

    book

11.

    France   These nouns are

    Alice   *_____ nouns.

    Bible

12.

                    Common nouns all start with a

                 *_____ letter.

13.

                    Proper nouns all start with a

                 *_____ letter.

14.

    Potomac   Two of these words are proper nouns.

    river   Write their names here:

    planet

    Mars   *_____

15.

    Beatles   Two of these words are common nouns.

    band   Write their names here:

    Christmas

    holiday   *_____

---

10. common 11. proper 12. small 13. capital
14. Potomac, Mars 15. band, holiday

16.

tuesday	nation	
dog	germany	
city	indian	
state	april	
easter	pen	

Five of these words are proper nouns. Find these proper nouns and draw a line under the letter to be capitalized.

17.
Each of the sentences below has a proper noun. (If two words name one thing they are both capitalized). Find the proper noun(s) in each sentence and draw a line under the letter(s) to be capitalized.

It was cold that december day.

We sailed on the chesapeake bay.

My father reads the washington post.

His ancesters came over on the mayflower.

She lives at 711 oak street.

Composition can be taught by (1) imitation and (2) sub-vocalization. Imitation is simply copying with emphasis on details. Give your students sample paragraphs or letters to copy several times—until the form is fixed in their minds. Then, use the vanishing technique. Hand out a sample with one part missing which they are to supply. Follow this with two parts missing and so on until they must reconstruct from memory almost the entire paragraph.

Sub-vocalization is to convert a vocal description into writing. Have one of your students act out an episode. The

---

16. Tuesday, Easter, Germany, Indian, April
17. December, Chesapeake Bay, Washington Post,
Mayflower, Oak Street.

class is instructed to describe to themselves what he has done. They then tell orally what they saw. When you are satisfied that they can narrate accurately what occured, have them write out the description, using simple, standard English and correct punctuation. The sequence would follow a prescribed order:

1. Observe action, saying to yourself what happened.
2. Tell what happened orally.
3. Write out what happened, using concrete details, action words, and sensory appeals.
4. Check punctuation with the text book.
5. Check spelling with the dictionary.
6. Re-write corrected paragraph until it is legible.

LITERATURE FOR SLOW LEARNERS

Style, symbolism, the masterful rhetoric of great writers, all are lost on slow learners. Even if it were possible to find a way to make them appreciate such unique talent, the accomplishment would be of little use to them in later life. The time expended can be used to better advantage. The slow learner can, however, learn to comprehend the great truths of human nature, particularly as they pertain to the emotions. This can best be done through the use of films. Many films are available, the themes of which are rich in complex human relationships, notably those dealing with the family. Slow learners, aided by the teacher, can easily identify with the characters in the story and become conscious of the factors behind their own behavior and that of their neighbors. Many fine short films are also available, either free or at a low rental cost.[21]

---

[21] Consult Association Films, Inc. Executive Offices, 600 Madison Ave. New York, N.Y. 10022. Write for catalogue.

An excellent way to better channel the natural interest of slow learners in television is to have the class select a committee to study the TV Guide in advance and recommend programs for viewing. If class discussions are held after the showing and extra points awarded for actual participation, worthwhile programs will fill tremendous gaps in the student's knowledge of the world. Let the committee, under your guidance, handle the entire lesson. You will be amazed at the good judgment they will show, even when it is not the same as yours.

TEACHING STANDARD ENGLISH FOR APPROPRIATE OCCASIONS

Non-standard English expressions occur frequently in both the speech and writing of slow learners and disadvantaged children. Some of the most common are:

1. *Combining past and present tense in the same sentence:*
   "I went to the library and I checks out this book."
   "She asks me, was I ever going to finish talking."
2. *Improper, or no antecedent for pronouns:*
   "She shot her when she went to her store for her groceries."
3. *Omitting the verb entirely:*
   "He right." "You mistaken."
   "They happy." "They married."
4. *Subject and verb do not agree:*
   "They looks for the money, and they finds it in their purses."
5. *Repetition of the subject:*
   "That man, he cheats everybody."

These are expressions disadvantaged children hear daily in their homes and communities. They use them to communicate with parents and neighbors. Trying to break them of this idiom would leave them tongue-tied. They can, however, be taught to use standard English in appropriate situations. This cannot be taught by text books or work books. It must be learned orally. First, record their speech and select the expressions which need to be corrected. Then, tape the desired construction and pronounciation. Do not make this stilted or use words they will never need. Keep it simple, pronounce it slowly and distinctly with emphasis on endings. Play this tape for short periods each day while they listen. When the pattern becomes familiar, let them pronounce after the tape for a number of times. Finally, let them tape their own speech and compare it with yours. Better yet, find a student who does speak standard English and have him make your tapes.

This may be a slow process, but it can be successful if you persist. When they can say standard English orally, have them write it a number of times so that the oral pattern becomes translated into a visual pattern. Finally, hold short discussions in the class each day in which only standard English is permitted. They will thus become accustomed to switching from their idiom to standard English when the situation is appropriate.

chapter 8

Teaching Mathematics to the Slow Learner

To be precise in answering the question of what mathematics the slow learner needs, the only candid reply would be, all he can learn. At the barest minimum, he must be able to handle wisely his personal finance and daily living requirements such as: payroll deductions, taxes, insurance, banking, installment buying, family budgeting, measurement, labels and recipes; but equally important are employment demands that increasingly necessitate mathematics. The following jobs, suitable for slow learners, call for several years of high school math, merging into algebra and geometry: bank and billing clerk, bookkeeper, carpenter, practical nurse, electrician, mechanic, plumber, sales clerk, secretary, and all technical positions. Yet, experience warns that, as presently taught, algebra and geometry are almost impossible for slow learners to pass. Whether different methods of teaching these subjects would enable slow learners to understand them is an open question. The fact remains, that at present, in spite of the "new math," slow learners are falling further and further behind in needed quantitative ability.

In the fall of 1969, the author made a survey of 374

ninth graders entering the freshmen class of the school in which he was employed. All had taken the Differential Aptitude Test Battery in the eighth grade. This battery yields a score in both verbal and numerical aptitudes. Exactly what comprises the numerical aptitude which the test measures is difficult to say, but presumably, past instruction would effect the score significantly. The test is widely given and correlates well with other tests of the same nature. The author found 62% of the ninth graders scoring below the 50th percentile on numerical ability. More significant, 47% scored below the 30th percentile, yet almost all of these students made verbal scores at least 15% higher. There is nothing normal about this distribution, particularly so, since these students came from a predominately middle class neighborhood. Moreover, the school system and teachers rank among the best in the nation. The inescapable conclusion is that, although the upper 38% may have learned well, the lower 47% are woefully inept in numerical ability.

THE NEW MATH CURRICULA
FOR SLOW LEARNERS

It is quite likely that the instruction of these ninth graders was suitable only to those students who grasped symbolism and abstractions easily and who were competent readers. Mathematicians who write books and math teachers who have spent years studying the subject are apt to take for granted that statements and principles simple to them are equally understandable to children.

Take for example, the following, typical of the wording of the new math in ninth grade text books: "In a given computation entailing a variable, the variable is a numeral which represents a definite, though unspecified number, from a given set of admissible numbers." Very probably, a slow learner encountering this sentence would immediately decide this was incomprehensible to him and that further effort on his part would be futile. An understanding teacher might have saved him by explaining: "Look—it's like this. The manager of the Mets is planning his strategy for the game next Saturday. For his lineup he puts down eight names, but because of injuries, he doesn't know who he will start at first base, so he puts down an X for the ninth name. This X could stand for any one of five players. This X is a variable. Using it he can go ahead and plan his strategy. You too can solve a problem using an X (a variable) to stand for a number you don't know." But how many understanding teachers exist, and if they do, how many have the time or patience to devote to slow learners. If they did, they would probably not have time to finish the text book by the end of the semester, and their college bound students would not score well on the college boards. All of this means that the slow learner is low man on the totem pole.

Many schools and teachers are well aware of this problem. Ruth Irene Hoffman, professor of mathematics at the University of Denver, states in 'The Slow Learner—Changing His View of Math":[1] "Fear of mathematics and a distaste for any computation or for the kind of analytical thinking that typifies mathematics—these qualities characterize the slow learner in mathematics. This fear and distaste are born most frequently of some early fuzzy understanding or misunderstanding and are nurtured in succeeding years by the frustration of attempting to build new understandings on a nonexistant foundation."

One organization with an answer to this problem is called CAMP (Concepts and Applications of Mathematics Project), under the direction of Paul C. Rosenbloom of Teachers College, Columbia University. A *Project Conference*

---

[1] Hoffman, Ruth Irene. *The Coming Revolution in Mathematics.* Reprinted from the Bulletin of National Association of Secondary School Principals. No. 327. April 1968 for the National Council of Teachers of Mathematics. 1201 Sixteenth St. N.W. Washington, D.C.

Report[2] contains many valuable suggestions for teaching math to slow learners. The major concepts advocated by this group are:

1. *The Mathematics Laboratory*—This has already been described in previous chapters, but it may further be defined as "a state of mind." The physical plant will include multisensory aids such as overhead projectors, film strips, movie projectors, measuring devices, and calculators; but the basic goal is to improve the student's attitude toward mathematics by presenting number concepts in several different contexts and employing as many different senses as possible.

2. *Flow Charting*—This is a logical device to analyze a problem and break it down into its basic operations. It can start with non-mathematical situations such as: "Tying your shoe" or "Cooking Oatmeal" and precede to simple algorithms. This presents problem solving in an understandable fashion. A sample flow chart is illustrated on page 185. The flow chart forces children to answer such questions as:

   a) What facts are needed?

   b) What is the first step in solving this problem?

   c) What steps will follow and in what order?

   d) What will be the final result?

4. *The Electric Printing Calculator*—Its function is not to bypass computation but to reinforce it. The calculator teaches decimal point location, estimation, discovery of the interrelationship of basic computation, checks the work done by hand, and familiarizes the student with the latest equipment used by business. Slow learners are intrigued by the machines and their ability to use them enhances their self-respect.

As an example, the slow learner, in order to set up a division problem on the calculator, must recognize the process as repeated subtraction. This is probably the first time he has ever understood what he was doing when he divided.

---

[2] CAMP. *Project Conference Report,* held April 21-22 at Central College, Pella, Iowa. 50219. Send 35c to the above address.

FLOW CHART FOR GETTING UP IN THE MORNING

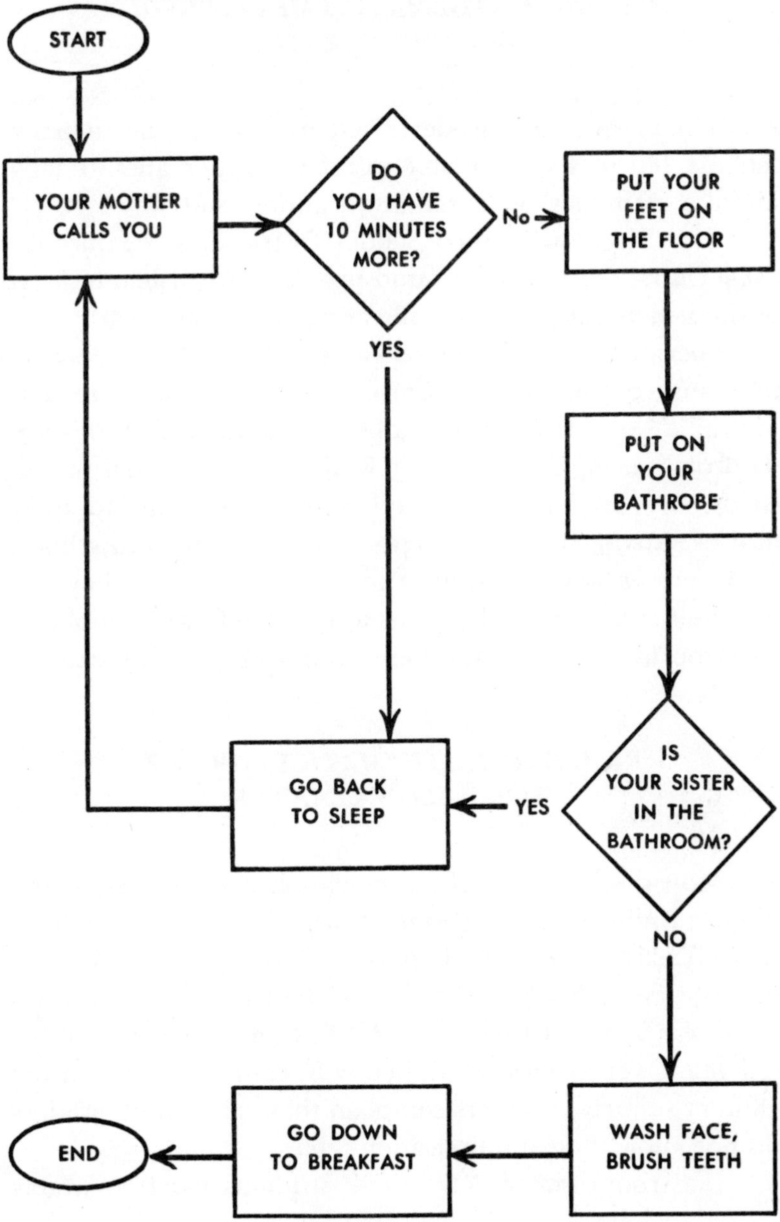

MAKING MATHEMATICS MEANINGFUL
TO SLOW LEARNERS

The innovations just described are not available to many schools, but it is still possible to relate mathematics to daily life in a manner slow learners will understand.

The Stockton Unified School District has organized a *Math Curriculum Guide*[3] around problems furnished by local businessmen. Each problem illustrates some basic mathematical operation such as: place value, decimals, ratio, whole numbers, estimation, fractions, addition, subtraction and multiplication of rational numbers. Scheduled with this are daily drills using the EDL Math Builder, Math Mate with film strips, overhead projector and 30 mm projector to show movies. Any part of this program can be adopted by schools anywhere. Allowing children to understand how they will use the math they are learning when they finish school and enter business illuminates their math lessons with meaning.

REMEDIAL MATHEMATICS FOR THE
OLDER SLOW LEARNER

Most discouraging of all to schools and teachers is the plight of ninth and tenth graders whose knowledge of math scarcely exceeds the fourth grade. It has been estimated that in large city schools 50% of the student body falls into this category. Some of these students have attended school for ten years, yet experience difficulty in counting. Even in the affluent suburbs, teachers complain that many ninth graders do not know their multiplication tables.

Classroom material for these students must be largely

---

[3] *Math Curriculum Guide.* California State Department of Education, Stockton Unified School District, Stockton, California.

teacher constructed. Text books of basic math used in elementary schools would only insult slow learners. To avoid monotony, a variety of materials is necessary. Using the same text day after day quickly turns them off. Nor does their attention span permit them to work over the same problem until they get it right. Lessons must be kept simple, socially mature, and diversified. Three or more changes of method are required for each fifty minute period. Excellent suggestions can be found in issues of *The Mathematics Teacher*.[4]

Tapes for short drills can be purchased or can be made locally. One teacher found that when students concentrated on what comes over the head phones, they learned three times faster than by using text books and chalk board demonstrations. If visual representation of the material accompanies the tape, sight further reinforces comprehension. It may often be necessary to tape explanations for the benefit of non-readers and to expand these tapes to include oral responses by the students.

Some programmed materials are available, but most suffer from frames that non-readers cannot digest. One notable exception is *Programmed Math for Adults*[5] written by Sullivan Associates.

Self-contained lessons which can be completed by the end of the period and immediately evaluated have proven the most satisfactory. Slow learners have a dreary history of failure and need the chance to succeed daily. To achieve this goal, lessons must proceed in small steps which slow learners can comprehend and thus experience a feeling of success. No pressure should be exerted to induce them to complete the daily exercise. If proper conditions have been effected, they will do this on their own. Frequent short, simple tests, which they can correct themselves, will prove excellent

---

[4] Official journal of the National Council of Teachers of Mathematics. 1201 Sixteenth St. N.W. Washington, D.C.
[5] Published by McGraw-Hill Book Co. 330 42nd St., New York, N.Y.

morale builders by demonstrating to them they have made progress.

Homework is practically useless, for when they encounter something they do not understand, they quit work. Moreover, they receive little reinforcement from it since they are unable to discover if they have the correct answers until the following day when the learning effect has been lost. Games and puzzles, however, can be checked out by individuals or groups to take home.

As in all other school work, the teacher is the most important factor. No matter how profound her grasp of mathematics, if the teacher cannot communicate with the pupil she is a failure. Many mathematics teachers seem overly concerned with maintaining standards, often at the expense of common sense. When teaching slow learners, it is pertinent to inquire as to whose standards are being upheld and for what purpose. Without condoning time wasting or deliberate indifference on the part of students, teachers can patiently repeat simple, but fundamental processes, at a pace slow learners can absorb, until these processes become a part of the student's thinking. The pace at which learning takes place will undoubtedly be speeded if grades are assigned for progress, rather than upon the attainment of some arbitrary standard.

A workable classroom program that can be employed follows:

1. Determine the level at which each individual is operating. Several good diagnostic tests are available,[6] but it is not difficult for teachers to design one themselves.

2. Start each pupil at his lowest level of difficulty. If he cannot divide fractions, he starts at this point and works at his own speed

---

[6] Comprehensive tests of Basic Skills—Arithmetic Test. California Test Bureau. McGraw-Hill Book Co. Hightstown, N.J.

Stanford Diagnostic Arithmetic Test. Harcourt Brace & World Test Department. 757 Third Ave. New York, N.Y.

Basic Skills in Arithmetic. Science Research Associates, Inc. 259 East Erie St. Chicago, Ill.

until he has mastered this one task. From there he will embark on a sequential course in basic math that slowly increases in difficulty. He does not move on to this next chore until he has mastered the one he is working on. He will require considerable indvidual help, and where teacher's aides are employed, their services will be invaluable. Understanding comes hard to the older slow learner and he is easily discouraged. Better students can be of great assistance to the weaker.

3. Divide the class into small groups, each working at different levels or tasks. They can help each other while the teacher moves about giving assistance. As soon as a student can pass a test which shows he has mastered the group task, he moves to another group.

4. Avoid monotony by capitalizing on problems which are handy and thus meaningful to students.

5. Help your students to be wise consumers by instructing them in a course of personal mathematics which any teacher can devise. A most useful booklet for this purpose is *Curriculum Resource Materials For Meeting School Retention and Pre-Employment Needs,*[7] published by the Board of Education, City of New York.

Vocational mathematics is best taught in conjunction with the trade or skill the student is learning. Not only will it be more useful to him on the job, but he will easily see its meaning when he can use it for a practical purpose.

---

[7] Board of Education of the City of New York, Publication Sales Office, 110 Livingston Street, Brooklyn, N.Y. $1.50. Make checks payable to Auditor, Board of Education.

chapter 9

Some Suggestions for Teaching Social Studies and Science to Slow Learners

Social studies is one branch of school curricula that can be taught better without a text book so that little modification of instruction is needed to make it adaptable to slow learners, yet it is a vital area often neglected. Such a wealth of audio-visual material is becoming available that the teaching of social studies need never again be dull.

The social revolution gathering momentum around the world lends urgency to the preparation of the slow learner to deal with social problems from as complete a knowledge of history, geography, and sociology as possible. Sooner or later, he must calculate his own stake in the conflicting ideologies. He, more than students of the upper socio-economic class, is apt to be caught-up in any struggle, both emotionally and economically. While the radical elements in this nation belong largely to the intellectual class, strenuous efforts are being made to involve labor and the minority groups. A serious recession in the nation's economy could easily weld these groups into a revolutionary base with great power. Many slow learners and disadvantaged youth would identify quickly with such a movement.

On the other hand, an even greater danger exists that the excesses of the activist left will unite the silent majority of middle class working men, farmers, professionals and businessmen into a conservative coalition to combat lawlessness. Such a movement might easily expand into a police state. Strangely enough, the ruthless power needed to maintain such structure would possess a fascination for many slow learners who would understand its terrible simplicity better than the intellectual ferment of the campuses.

From a practical standpoint, the lower socio-economic class could gain little from a clash of these forces. Any disruption of the delicate balance of our society would fall hardest upon those with meager resources. Slow learners, usually falling into this category, would inevitably suffer the greatest hardships. For this reason, they must understand what is happening in our society and why it is taking place. Most of all, they must be aware of the resources available to them short of violence to better their position in society.

A second important reality to be learned through social studies is the increasing internationalism of the world. From early childhood, students must be taught the kinship of all peoples and the obligation of each race and nation to promote tolerance, brotherhood and cooperation. Only when such knowledge is widespread can racism and the insane nationalism that feeds war be brought under control.

A third danger area is communication—the torrent of words that pours over us daily, seeking to persuade, to excite, to coax, to bully, to deceive. The slow learner is easily swayed by the subtle nuances of propaganda until sour tastes sweet and falsehood becomes truth. With his limited comprehension of words he can easily be led by those seeking power to betray his own interests. Only through the lessons of history can he perceive the fearsome struggle and cost by which his ancestors have purchased his freedom, a struggle still going on. Some facts need to be repeated over and over. For example, he needs to be constantly reminded that although some idealogies may sound attractive, the citizens of nations now practicing them must be restrained by force from fleeing by the millions.

Fourth, and most puzzling of all, is the current menace of nihilism. Bewildered by the intricacy of modern life, cast adrift from traditional values and the security of ancestral dogmas, young people in increasing numbers are turning to a simpler way of life, a renunciation of society's conventions, hygiene, moral codes, and dress. While a spiritual renaissance is long overdue, even a slight acquaintance with sociology and economics confirms that an involved society under the pressure of population explosion cannot return to a pastoral age. History paints a grim picture of the struggle of primitive man to wring a bare subsistence from the soil and to conquer disease and plague. By contrast, man's present triumph over his environment holds a glittering promise for his future if he can only discipline himself enough to grasp it rather than seek escape in the embrace of null values.

Personal decisions, growing out of the foregoing social dilemmas, will gravely effect the lives of today's students. Nothing the school can teach will overshadow the seriousness of these issues as they are resolved, yet schools shy away from such subjects as being too controversial. It often seems that education regards using the proper antecedent for a pronoun or memorizing a passage from "Le Morte d'Arthur" as of more importance than acquiring attitudes, values and ethics. As a result, the inexperienced youth is left to formulate his own values without guidance. For some time, schools have been "hung up" on a meaningless phrase which states. "Values must be caught—not taught." Caught how? Like a cold? By that time it is too late.

Social studies teachers have an opportunity and an obligation to open up for discussion and evaluation real issues confronting youth today. When they do, they are amazed at the eagerness with which students welcome a chance to clarify their doubts and misgivings.

TEACHING SOCIAL STUDIES IN ELEMENTARY SCHOOL

From the time he enters school, the child must learn to feel a common bond with children of other races and nations. One of the best means of accomplishing this is through folk songs. There is a basic simplicity and rhythm about folk singing that has universal appeal, particularly to the slow learner. Their flavor of social living acquaints children with strange settings and foreign cultures. Hunting songs, lullabies, counting songs, hymns, patriotic songs, and minstrel tunes all teach children that all peoples have common goals, desires, joys, and sorrows. A useful source for obtaining and using folk songs is *How to Use Folk Songs*.[1]

Sociodrama is a second useful device for younger students including slow learners who love to act out a problem in social relations just as people would in real life. Role-playing has always been successful with slow learners of all ages. It helps them to identify with other types of personalities, to see points of view differing from their own, and to analyze conflicting human interests in highly emotional situations. Such social skills and desirable attitudes as responsibility, cooperation, loyalty, honesty, fairness, and respect for the beliefs and customs of others can be self-taught in an understandable fashion.

---

[1] *How to Use Folk Songs.* No. 25—"How To Do It Series". Price 25c. National Council for the Social Studies. National Education Association. 1201 16th St. N.W. Washington, D.C.

Useful suggestions for using sociodrama can be found in *How to use Sociodrama.*[2]

There are three basic types of sociodrama:

1. *The Daily Living Problem*—which students themselves recognize as existing in the school, on the playground and in the family. This is easily the most fascinating to them, since they choose the topic in which they have a vital interest and which effects the largest majority of them.

2. *The Fictitious Story*—This relates to the larger society which may be outside of their immediate sphere of experience but to which students can relate because of its human qualities. Here the teacher selects the topic for study and attempts to relate it to the interests of the pupils.

3. *The Political or Social Question*—This is more suitable for older students who will need to be supplied background material from newspapers, books, films, or field trips. It is possible to dramatize historical events and social issues of both past and present quite vividly if students have been properly prepared.

As early in school as possible, a child must begin to orient himself in relation to his environment. This is best done through the use of maps and globes. The first grade is none too early to teach such social studies skills as direction, the concept of up and down, and relative distances. Children are most likely to see usefulness in maps when they are gaining some geographic knowledge such as a representation of their own neighborhood. This can gradually be expanded to include cities, states, nations, the globe and space. A useful technique is to have children report on trips they have taken while the class traces the route on the map.

Maps are not difficult for slow learners to comprehend, but the symbolic language they employ must be taught slowly

---

[2] *How to Use Sociodrama.* No. 20—"How To Use It Series". 25c. National Council for the Social Studies. National Education Association. 1201 16th St. N.W. Washington, D.C.

and meaningfully. A useful resource for this purpose is *How to Introduce Maps and Globes—Grades One Through Six*.[3]

Pictures, slides, film strips, tapes, and colored transparencies are available from many sources[4] to supplement both folksongs and map studies. Most of these are new and well-made, bringing a colorful window on the world into the classroom. A creative teacher with color film can soon build up a catalogue of slides showing historical spots, slums, factories, objects of culture, and sporting events in her own neighborhood or from wherever she travels on vacations.

A complete new series of booklets, well-illustrated, with language suitable for slow learners in primary grades, called *Man in Action*,[5] has a fine inter-disciplinary approach to human endeavor.

TEACHING SOCIAL STUDIES IN MIDDLE SCHOOL

Most of the techniques already mentioned can be carried over into middle school. The depth of presentation will depend upon the level at which students are working. Since very little reading is involved, the interest and maturity level of the class will dictate the teacher's approach. Care must be taken that the contributions of all minority races comprising our nation are given their proper weight; not as separate studies, but as an integral part of our history which all children need to know. The purpose for this is to bring to all students the common heritage all Americans share.

Two techniques, highly suitable for middle school slow

[3] *How to Introduce Maps and Globes—Grades One Through Six* "How To Do It Series"—No. 15. 25c. National Council for the Social Studies. National Education Association. 1201 16th St. N.W. Washington, D.C.
[4] Creative Visuals. John Glisson. 819 Broad St. Richmond, Va.
Society for Visual Education. 1345 Deversey Parkway, Chicago, Ill. 60614.
Nystrom. 3333 Elston Ave. Chicago, Illinois. 60618.
Woolensak Teaching Tapes. Mincom Division. 3M Center. St. Paul, Minnesota. 55101.
[5] Educational Book Division. Prentice Hall. Englewood Cliffs, N.J. 07632.

learners and particularly for disadvantaged children are the "field trip" and recordings.

Children in impoverished neighborhoods and in isolated, rural areas live in drab ignorance of the exciting world outside their immediate neighborhoods or community. All children need closer acquaintance with the realities of society. Slow learners in particular need concrete experience to see meaning in what they are learning.

Every community is a microcosm of society, and most schools lie within travelling distance of a large city where the same picture can be seen on a grand scale. It is dangerous to keep children unaware of the complexity of our society. The importance of the continued health and smooth operation of our governmental and economic system to their own lives often seems not appreciated. All too many live in a vacuum, apparently unaware that reckless tampering with laws and economics can bring down the entire structure on their own heads. Direct contact with life will help them to see it as real, not the world they view in detachment through a television screen.

Desirable places to visit are: banks, factories, communication and transportation centers, governmental agencies, places of historical interest, cultural and recreational opportunities. A pamphlet useful to social studies teachers is *How to Utilize Community Resources.*[6]

Just as films are an eye on the world, so recordings are an ear on history. Tape recordings and transcriptions, used in conjunction with maps, film strips, and photographs provide vivid lessons for slow learners. Recordings not only improve listening skills, but promote acquaintance with famous personalities and give children the feeling they were present during climactic past events.

---

[6] *How to Utilize Community Resources.* No. 13—"How To Do It Series." 25c. National Council for the Social Studies. National Education Association. 1201 16th St. N.W. Washington, D.C.

For poor readers, no instructional media is as effective as the *I Can Hear it Now* (Columbia Records) albums and the *You Are There* programs, a life-like CBS Series released on Columbia Records. It is possible for students to be present at the signing of the Magna Carta, the Battle of Gettysburg and many other historical events. A complete listing of available recordings can be found in *How to Use Recordings.*[7]

For social studies teachers in search of texts suitable for slow learners, the *Follet Basic Learning Programs*[8] have simple formats and reading levels as low as the fourth grade, but with adult interest.

TEACHING SOCIAL STUDIES IN THE HIGH SCHOOL

Three areas of social studies have meaning and importance to slow learners in high school. These are American History, current events, and the operation of local government. Unfortunately, the text books used in most schools to teach American history and American government (two subjects required for a diploma) are too difficult for most slow learners to read. American government is singularly dry and confusing, particularly when it is taught (as usual) by reading assignment plus lecture. Only teacher-constructed material can make it come to life. There is much that is irrelevant to the needs of slow learners in both subjects as they are presently taught. What they actually need to know is:

1. The fundamental principles of democratic government.
2. The philosophy of individual freedom.
3. A knowledge of the struggle their ancestors have waged to preserve and expand civil liberty.

---

[7] *How to Use Recordings.* No. 8—"How To Do It Series." 25c National Council for the Social Studies. American Education Association. 1201 16th St. N.W. Washington, D.C.

[8] *Social Studies Programs for the Slow Learner.* Follet Educational Corporation. 1010 W. Washington St. Chicago, Illinois 60607.

4. The basis of the strength, security and prosperity of the United States and how it compares with that of other nations.
5. The obligations required of each individual citizen if this heritage is to be preserved and projected into the future.
6. The nature of events and forces existing in the world today that may effect their own future.
7. The operation of governmental agencies that immediately effect their own lives.

In teaching American history without textbooks, the exploitation of two assets is most helpful. They are films and local history. A generation whose umbilical cord plugs into the television is uniquely conditioned to learning by sound and picture. The film, using animation, slow-motion, and time-lapse photography, can produce effects impossible with any other media. In historical reinactments, films recapture the local color and settings of another age. Used in conjunction with recordings, history comes alive for non-readers as in no other technique. Moreover, the ability to replay films stimulates discussion and allows for clarification of issues, lending interest and variety to classroom work. For maximum benefits from films, careful preparation and follow-up by the teacher is necessary in order to involve students themselves in the lesson.

A great mass of film is available, so much that considerable time is required to select those which are most appropriate. All motion pictures should be previewed in order to cull out those films which attempt to promote a cause or sell a commodity or service. A valuable aid to the teacher in locating sources of film is *How to Use A Motion Picture.*[9]

Past history often seems so remote to the "now" generation that they confuse it with fiction. For this reason, traditions and heritage become more meaningful if students can see the changes taking place in their own community. The

[9] *How to Use a Motion Picture.* No. 1—"How To Do It Series." 25c. National Council for the Social Studies. National Education Association. 1201 16th St. N.W. Washington, D.C.

resulting continuity links them with the receding past and provides better understanding of community problems which leads to better citizenship. Historical societies and museums exist in every community. The files of the local newspaper contain fascinating photographs, advertisements, and gossip, colorful trivia which have already been lost to text books. Areas to be explored by the class are politics, buildings, transportation, communication, real estate, and occupations. A useful resource for teachers is *How to Use Local History.*[10]

Social studies teachers need to develop in every student the practice of reading the daily papers. As never before, all citizens must keep knowledgeable of current events. Fortunately, the daily paper is highly suitable to the reading level and interests of the slow learner.

An important educational task is to emphasize critical reading, so that the student may discuss contemporary events sensibly and base his actions on enlightened judgment. It is desirable that more than one newspaper be used in the classroom, so that conflicting opinions and biased reporting be detected and correctly evaluated. Newspapers are best employed as a daily part of classroom work. Student committees can be formed to take over certain daily tasks such as keeping bulletin boards and situation maps. The teacher's chore is to tie the daily news to the long prospective of history. Of value to teachers in this duty is *How to Use Daily Newspapers.*[11]

Scholastic Magazines[12] has two current affairs magazines for classroom use, in addition to *Scope* which is written chiefly for slow learners. They are *Junior Scholastic,* with a reading

---

[10] *How to Use Local History.* No. 3—"How To Do It Series." 25c National Council for the Social Studies. National Education Association. 1201 16th St. N.W. Washington, D.C.

[11] *How to Use Daily Newspapers.* No. 5—"How To Do It Series." Ibid.

[12] Scholastic Magazines, Inc. 902 Sylvan Ave. Englewood Cliffs, New Jersey. 07632.

level of grades 6-8, and *World Week,* with a reading level of grades 9-10. A second supplier of classroom news periodicals is American Education Publications. [13]

Paperback multi-texts, film strips, and colored transparencies on current affairs are available from several publishers. [14]

An ingenious teacher can devise many understandable ways of presenting such necessary subjects as voting rights, consumer economics, local politics, etc. Those interested should secure the February 1970 issue of *Social Studies.* [15] The entire issue is about slow learners. Also valuable will be *New Social Studies for the Slow Learner.* [16]

TEACHING SCIENCE TO THE SLOW LEARNER

It is doubtful if many slow learners will become scientists. The technical professions, so essential to scientific and engineering, are more suitable for them. One reason for this is the fact that such subjects as chemistry, physics, and higher levels of biology are too abstract. The theoretical mathematics necessary for mastery of these subjects is beyond the grasp of slow learners. The question as to whether different methods of teaching would overcome this handicap awaits some breakthrough in learning theory. The prospects for this are dim, since it would be a matter of the tail chasing the dog. Mathematics is constantly ascending into the rarefied atmosphere in which only the gifted can breathe.

This does not imply that slow learners have no need for

---

[13] American Education Publications. Education Center, Columbus, Ohio, 43216.

[14] Popular Science Publishing Co., Inc. Audio Visual Division. 355 Lexington Ave., New York, N.Y. 10017.

Childrens Press, Inc. 1224 West Van Buren, Chicago, Ill.

[15] Social Education. Vol. 34 No. 2 February 1970. National Council for the Social Studies. 1201 16th St. Washington, D.C.

[16] *The New Social Studies for the Slow Learner.* Social Studies Curriculum Center Carnegie-Mellon University.

science. Their future will be largely shaped by science. To name a few problems to which they must make adjustments and contributions—all scientifically oriented: ecology (maintaining a healthy environment for mankind), medical advances to conquer disease and prolong life, space travel, computer technology, and electronic communication. Slow learners must be aware of the impact these discoveries have on society. Above all, they must understand the scientific methods being used to revolutionize man's knowledge of his environment.

Science text books have come under considerable criticism because of their arduous prose, often a grade or more above even the average student's level. Text books, however, are the poorest method of teaching science, and there is no longer need for their use with slow learners. Film strips, motion pictures and color transparencies are available for teaching almost every area of science in a way even slow learners can comprehend.[17] Multi-texts, designed particularly for slow learners, are also published on the 5-6 grade level.[18] Even more useful in the elementary school are complete classroom laboratories which children can use themselves to demonstrate basic scientific principles.[19] A simple and intelligible method of teaching physiology is the use of mock-ups. Life-size and even larger models of human organs, bones and body parts can be obtained, which can be taken apart and reassembled.[20]

For the high school, the Biological Sciences Curriculum Study—Special Materials, has been uniquely designed for

---

[17] Society for Visual Education, Inc. Op Cit.
Creative Visuals. Op Cit.
D.C. Heath. Malalaster Scientific Division. Raytheon Education Co. 285 Columbus Ave., Boston, Mass. 02116.
[18] Globe Book Co., Inc. 175 Fifth Ave., New York, N.Y. 10010.
[19] Harcourt, Brace & World. Op Cit.
[20] Denoyer-Geppert. Times Mirror, 5235 Ravenswood Ave. Chicago, Illinois 60640.

use with slow learners, not only to teach ecological principles, but to initiate students into the scientific method of inquiry. The contents and methods employed in teaching this course have already been described in Chapters 2 and 5. When the teacher's handbook is strictly followed, no student need fail. One danger is that teachers cannot resist the temptation to upgrade the materials to meet their own standards, thus squeezing out the slow learners once again.

Scholastic Magazines, Inc.[21] have recently introduced a classroom periodical called *Science World.* One section is written specifically for slow learners. A worthwhile source of material for teachers is *Science and Children* for elementary science pupils and *The Science Teacher* for secondary school science pupils, both publications of National Science Teachers Association.[22]

---

[21]Scholastic Magazines, Inc. Op Cit.
[22]National Science Teachers Association, 1201 16th St. Washington, D.C. 20036.

chapter 10

Counseling the Slow Learner

The primary objective of counseling is to assist students to understand themselves through assessment of their interests, aptitudes, achievements, abilities, and personality characteristics and to make wise use of these data to plan their vocational, educational, and personal goals. For most students, the counselor can perform this function with reasonable confidence. Not so with slow learners. Until the emotional distortions which block awareness can be reduced, all other aims are futile. To venture past this point, the counselor must abandon his safe and familiar role and be guided solely by his instinct. It is a gamble that requires a special breed.

WHO CAN COUNSEL SLOW LEARNERS?

If you are willing to counsel the slow learner, you must first equip yourself with certain emotional mental sets.

1. You must be willing to put aside your own values, which are meaningless to him, but resist being seduced by his values into condoning self-destructive behavior in hope of achieving camaraderie. Your sympathy for him must not obscure reality.

2. You must be unflappable—that is—you must have enough

self-confidence to venture into situations, the outcome of which you cannot foresee.

3. You must endeavor to enter his world—to understand his point of view without repugnance. If you feel reproof he will sense it.

4. You must have sufficient maturity and dignity not to be repelled by youthful hostility or ridicule.

5. You must have a calm, warm personality, a genuine liking for young people, and a total absence of rigidity in dealing with them.

6. You must be able to accept criticism and the opposition of some of your colleagues without abandoning your own convictions.

7. You must not fear to involve yourself emotionally in his life whenever necessary. He may need to lean on your experience, knowledge, and ego strength. He will not believe your expressed interest in him until you demonstrate it concretely.

8. You must be willing to listen patiently for long periods of time but speak positively when the situation demands.

9. You must resist fixing the blame for his problems solely on parents, teachers, police, or even society. It is not your business to fix blame. Very few people in his life are malicious. Most of them will think they are doing right from their own point of view. Living has always been complicated and difficult, particularly the creation and maintenance of a family. Mistakes are made from the best of intentions. You are certainly not wise enough to judge others.

10. You must be able to absorb the emotional impact of your own mistakes and defeats without serious damage to your courage.

The following, almost incredible story is true. Except for minor changes to protect identities, it can be completely authenticated.

The Case of Larry

Larry, a tall, blonde youth, so delicate that tiny red and blue veins spidered his face, was a junior in high school when referred to Mr. Foster, the counselor, for excessive absenteeism.

A study of Larry's file by Mr. Foster revealed that an abrupt change in school behavior had occurred during the ninth grade. Prior to that year, his grades had been excellent, and his test scores indicated a high degree of intelligence. He had missed 20 days during the ninth grade and 27 days the following year. In spite of this, he had passed all subjects.

The current year's outlook was more gloomy. With the semester barely half over, he had missed 20 days and was failing three subjects. A survey of his teachers elicited opinions varying from laziness to eccentric brilliance. All agreed that Larry appeared inattentive, argumentative, and non-conforming. Additionally, all commented on his aberrant hostility toward fellow students which provoked considerable scapegoating. He sought only the companionship of a few students, and those from minority races.

An unexpected outcome of the counselor's inquiry was an English theme brought in by an alarmed teacher. It was a brilliant defense of the civil rights movement but instead of employing moral and legal arguments, Larry had adopted a spiritual motif. The paper ended with a philosophical discourse on death, replete with mysticism.

Mr. Foster initiated a series of interviews with Larry which produced no results until the fifth session. At that time, for reasons of his own, Larry decided to reward the counselor's patience.

"I'm certain you mean well," Larry acknowledged. His manner was grave, his speech stilted, his words carefully chosen as though playing a role. There was a controlled strangeness about him, perplexing but ill-defined. "Unlike my teachers, you do not regard me as a 'kook'. I'm not—you know. As you see, I dress conservatively and can converse quite sensibly when I choose. I have already been to two psychiatrists who advised my father to let me alone to grow up—so to speak. Why don't you do the same?"

Mr. Foster nodded. "Then you won't mind if I speak to your father?"

"Not at all."

Larry's father, apparently a brilliant man, holding an important post with the United States Foreign Service, chain smoked and spoke with an Oxfordian accent.

"Is my son in difficulty?"

"He is failing several subjects and in danger of being suspended for non-attendance," Mr. Foster said.

"I see—has he spoken of our family problem?"

"No."

"Very well—I appreciate your concern—you should be informed." He drew a deep breath. "You see—several years ago, Larry's mother left me to live with a foreign student at a local university. The fellow is an Asian—apparently quite brilliant and sincere, although much younger than my wife. He practices some oriental religion—Zen—I believe. Larry was quite upset at the time but lately seems to have accepted the situation—enough to visit them occasionally. Larry lives with me. I provide him with all he needs, but there is very little communication between us. He goes off—I have no idea where—for several days at a time. I have sent him to several psychiatrists who advised me not to press matter with him. I shall speak to him about his school attendance. I would appreciate your continuing to talk with him."

The following day, Mr. Foster called Larry to his office. "Your father has told me about your mother," he said, "I'm sure you realize that your mother, like all of us, has the right to live her own life."

"Oh—quite—I have worked this out in my own mind some time ago."

"Good, now since you have been to several psychiatrists, I feel we should skip all psychological talk. Why don't we just talk about you—your school life—the here and now."

Larry nodded gravely. "Yes, that would be sensible. I've been giving some thought to that myself. I'm making rather a mess of things—am I not?"

"Oh—I wouldn't put it that drastically. There is nothing that can't be worked out. Why don't you give some thought to what you would like to do—then we can discuss your plans."

"That's an excellent suggestion. You will call me back next week?"

"Yes, unless you would like to see me before then. I'm always available, you know."

Larry was absent from school for the next two days. On the third day, two burly men walked into Mr. Foster's office. One produced a badge and a photograph. "Do you know this boy?"

"Why, yes, that's Larry Barton, but he's not in school today."

The man nodded. "We know—he's dead—set fire to himself in a patch of woods yesterday." Noting the shock on Mr. Foster's countenance, the detective seated himself heavily, waited for a moment, then spoke. "His father said you were his counselor. Do you know any reason he would do such a thing?"

"No-no," Mr. Foster whispered. "No—I don't know any reason. Was he drinking?"

"Perhaps, several empty beer cans were lying around."

School student bodies have a well-developed grapevine. They know who is pregnant and who broke into the liquor store before parents or police. They guard this information closely and stand together when one of them is in trouble.

As soon as he was able to pull himself together, Mr. Foster sent for the president of the junior class.

"I need some information, Tim, about a student."

Tim's eyes were wary. "Confidential, Mr. Foster?"

"Strictly confidential, Tim. "I want to know something about Larry Barton."

Tim nodded. "Terrible thing, wasn't it?"

"You know?"

"Yes, I heard last night."

"Was he on drugs, Tim?"

"He wasn't addicted. He sometimes carried it."

"Was he a homosexual?"

"No, I'm certain of that."

"Then, what was his hang-up?"

"We don't know, honestly, Mr. Foster. He was a loner. We thought you might know."

"No, Tim," Mr. Foster shook his head sadly. "No—I don't know."

On the way home that afternoon, Mr. Foster stopped at a bar and ordered a drink. This was unusual for him, since he hardly touched alcohol. Why? he thought, why? Larry had no insolvable problems. Why couldn't I have helped him? I know I got into it too late, but I don't understand it. What assurance do I have that I could have helped even earlier? All the years I spent at the

university—all the books I've read—all those wise,
bearded men who taught me. What do any of us know
about the minds of others. We're all a bunch of frauds. He
ordered a second drink.

Mr. Foster was late for supper that night and his wife
was very angry with him.

Many theories can be advanced about the cause of this
tragedy, but the true reason lies buried in the inscrutable
human mind. Counselors will be faced with many such
enigmas in the years to come. The social revolution sweep-
ing the world has strongly effected today's children. They
possess a tremendous urge to free themselves from the
control of others. This drive is charged with emotion and
does not yield to reason or reality. It defies one of mankind's
strongest taboos (against showing disrespect to parents)
and thus produces a burden of guilt that must be
exorcised by a powerful rationalization. One readily available
is the popular doctrine of existentialism which emphasizes
the importance of personal freedom, personal decision, and
personal commitment. Everyone must "do his own
thing."

This philosophy has great attraction for those who are
not "making it" in school. If all that is important is self-
expression, visible evidence of success is no longer necessary.
One is relieved from competition by proclaiming one's own
inner success. A new world is in the making and no return
to the old is possible, yet the technological and population explosions impose certain limitations on the future.
This book is not a forum for the discussion of the
merits of conformity, yet from a purely practical point of
view, the counselor is forced to point out that many of these
youths are in the wrong lane at rush hour, being in danger
of reaching middle age with no visible means of support.
There simply will not be that large a demand for guitar
players.

WHAT KIND OF COUNSELING IS EFFECTIVE?

Very few slow learners will seek your help unless you have acquired a reputation among students for being trustworthy, sympathetic, and effective. This means you must set about building such a reputation. Calling students to your office puts them immediately on guard, a handicap requiring time and patience to overcome.

Counseling must fit the student. An initial interview will be devoted largely to listening to his story, or, if the student is taciturn, to asking questions. After studying the student's file and seeking opinions from teachers, a tentative diagnosis of the nature of the problem can be made and a plan of action adopted.

The Genuine Slow Learner—He needs friendly support and reassurance. If he has no emotional problems, he responds well to counseling. You must give him reassurance that he can succeed in school and that you are going to help him do so. After you have committed yourself without reservations, you have no alternative but to make good on your promise. This means, usually, adjusting his subjects, schedules, and teachers; arranging for tutorial assistance and reading instruction; overseeing his assignments and classroom supplies; preping for his tests—even checking on his attendance. You may have to find him a part time job or help him get on the football squad. The system is stacked against him and it will require all of your clout to redress the balance.

The Behavior Problem—You will probably have to send for him or he will be sent to you. The cause of his behavior may soon be apparent to you, but usually there is little you can do about it. In most cases he will have to be taught new ways to react to his environment. For a long time it is best to talk about anything that interests him. If possible, just listen.

Avoid either condescension or a "now-you-know-that-is-no-way-to-act" attitude. Encourage him to express his point of view, but you dare not take his side against the faculty. He will exploit this. He must understand that you want to be a non-condemning friend but not an ally against the school system. You may do him favors, but let him understand this does not constitute approval of his behavior. Let him do errands for you to show him that you trust him. When he is in the bad graces of a teacher, let him stay in the guidance office for the day as a helper. Never become involved in his discipline. That will have to be handled by others.

Your relations may settle down to a long-term, friendly disagreement in which you both understand and respect each other's point of view. He badly needs a friend, and if you do not tune him out too early, he may come to regard you as one.

Reforming him may be impossible, but patience and persistence will afford you the opportunity to store his memory bank with useful responses to later conflicts. If you are lucky you may discover something that will provide him more recognition than his disruptive behavior, such as a part in a play or an active role as assistant to the physical education or shop teacher.

The Defeated—They have given up the struggle and now require massive support coupled with remedial assistance. In order to rebuild their ego strength, you may have to contrive some success, no matter how modest. It will require a cooperative effort on the part of teachers and parents and be a long, frustrating struggle. Since academic success is almost impossible, the school must turn to vocational success. One possible solution is to start them on vocational training as early as the eighth or ninth grade. If necessary, let them drop their academic program and concentrate only on vocational training. If they can become self-supporting, their ego strength may return.

The Emotionally Disturbed—Just listen to them for a long time. Talking releases their tension, and they will eventually tell you as much as they understand about their problem. At this point, you must decide whether their condition is beyond their knowledge and capability. If so, you must make every effort to secure the type of treatment they require. In cases where no outside assistance is available, you may continue your efforts. You are better than nothing and there is little danger you will make matters worse.

Some emotionally disturbed children attack their problems with senseless hostility—others seek escape through withdrawal—others stir up their environment randomly to release tension and anxiety. All of these are dead-end solutions. In rare cases you may improve the situation by working with the family. Where conditions are unalterable, you must attempt to persuade them to accept things as they are and learn to live with them. In nine out of ten cases this is quite possible, if only you can get them to see it. Hold out hope of escape if they will prepare themselves to be independent through education.

The Bright Underachiever—Here is a puzzle worthy of your skill. If you can win him over, you should write your own book.

There are no bright but lazy children. All have their own reasons for not achieving, although the reasons may not make sense to you. The numbers of bright underachieving children are increasing rapidly due to the present turmoil among the young as well as to the reinforcement they receive from certain intellectual circles. You will usually discover that the bright underachiever has a father or older sibling who has been very successful.

The bright underachiever is your intellectual equal and enjoys a contest of wits with you. He delights in obfuscation, in putting you on, in devising nonsensical games. If you become angry he will be amused. If you let him win, he loses interest in you. But fasten your seat belt—ride with him, and your reward will come years later. He will come back to visit you and say: "You'll never believe this, but:

"I want to be a teacher."

"I outrank my father."

"I'm credit manager of my father's Ford agency."

"I'm working for the Peace Corps."

"I'm probation officer for the juvenile court."

SHOWING THEM NEW WAYS TO REACT TO SCHOOL AND SOCIETY

Most problems brought to the counselor are caused by poor responses to home and society environmental conditions.

1. Often, all that is needed is a realistic reappraisal of themselves and a readjustment of their goals.
2. Often, they need only to accept family conditions as a fact and determine to live with a situation they cannot change.
3. Often, all they need is to stop blaming others and attempt to discover what they are doing wrong.
4. Often, they need only to accept the fact that they cannot have the world on their terms, but must make the most of the terms available.

It is not the gravity of their problems but their attitude toward them that makes their problems serious. Teachers, counselors and parents throw up their hands and lament: "He is so stubborn. If only he would listen." In that phrase lies the whole tragedy. He cannot hear the message. Slow learners must be shown, as well as told, how to act in their own self-interest. Counselors must show them how to study for particular tests, how to seek help from teachers, how to make friends, how to improve relations with parents, even how to get to school on time.

Some counselors will object at this point, "Those are minor problems. How do I show him how to kick the drug habit?" No one knows the answers to questions such as these. But get out of your office. Get to know him "'where he lives." When you know why he thinks he needs drugs, you might just be able to show him a better way to get his kicks, but under no circumstances attempt to treat drug addicts yourself. Get them to a physician without delay.

WORKING WITH PARENTS AND TEACHERS

It is your duty to work with parents if they are not hostile. In that case it is better not to antagonize them. Most parents are operating on insufficient data about their child's abilities, interests and aptitudes. Most are bewildered by their child's secretiveness. They are shocked when they find he has kept something from them or altered his grade on his report card. The counselor, projecting a different image of the child, can lead them to understand why the child felt the need to deceive them.

As a counselor, you should keep parents informed about their child's school record, grades, and test scores but not about his private affairs. Above all, never reveal, without his permission, confidences he has given you. In rare cases you must make a judgment as to whether the information you have about a child is potentially dangerous to him or to other children. If it is, you have an obligation to inform parents. Don't pretend to be wise enough to offer unsolicited advice to parents. Confine your counseling to matters you know about.

It is natural for a slight antagonism to develop between teachers and counselors, since it is always easier to sit in an office and tell someone what to do than to do it yourself. A good counselor will cultivate the friendship of teachers and establish a good working relationship. Above all, never do anything to lower a teacher's prestige in the eyes of the pupil. Much that you would like to accomplish can only be done with the cooperation of the teacher. Moreover, you need the teacher's viewpoint for better understanding of the child's response to his peer group in the classroom situation.

Unfortunately, you will occasionally encounter a teacher so insecure as to reject all of your suggestions. If this results in harm or injustice to the student, you have no recourse but to "lock horns with her." Every child is entitled to one ally in the school who will ensure that his grievances receive a fair hearing, and you are his ombudsman.

GROUP COUNSELING

Group counseling has already been touched upon in Chapter 5. It will never replace the one-to-one relationship of student and counselor, but it has one distinct advantage. It often succeeds with hard core deliquents where individual counseling fails. The reason for this success is the reinforcement deliquents receive from each other. Moreover, it is always easier to discern the inconsistencies in the attitude and behavior of others than in your own.

Face to face with the counselor, the deliquent assumes a sullen or mocking aloofness, but in a group, all of his bitterness wells over into verbal rancor. If you can ride out this tempest of accusations and ridicule, you will have earned his grudging respect. It is best to let the group tire of complaining before you even begin to reflect back their inconsistencies. Never lecture or moralize. Do not give advice unless asked. Confine yourself to guiding the discussion toward vocalizing unrealistic attitudes. Do not point out their self-deception. They need to recognize and acknowledge their own fallacies.

chapter 11

What the Future Holds

Although awareness of education is at an all-time
high, disillusionment with the nation's schools is wide spread.
This is largely due to the inability of educators to substantiate
results from large sums being expended by federal, state and
local governments. In February, 1970, U.S. Commissioner of
Education, James E. Allen, Jr., proposed the creation of a
new "National Institute of Education" to undertake a systematic search for new knowledge needed to make equal
educational opportunity a reality. Unless this search is di-
vorced from politics, academic theories, and social ideologies, its goal will prove more elusive than the landing on
Tranquility Base.

In spite of criticism, schools are moving forward in
attacking their problems and bright spots do appear.

1. The expansion of education downward to include
pre-school children will have great impact on the disadvantaged child. If he can be reached before his life style is
fixed, beneficial changes in behavior can be effected.

2. Many school systems are rewriting vocational curriculum with the aid of industry and labor unions in order to
make skill training more realistic. Such courses will be
unitary instructional modules including both the English and
mathematics necessary to successful employment.

3. Research, based on the studies of Swiss psychologist,

Jean Piaget, promises to benefit the education of slow
learners. Piaget claims that children progress through four
stages of learning. During each stage, they are able to absorb
different concepts and to assimilate different processes which
hasten advancement toward maturation. If optimum teaching techniques can be discovered to speed and amplify
natural capacity at each stage, more learning will take place.
Slow learners appear to lag behind average children in their
progression through the four stages.

4. Private clinics have been established in many cities to
develop perceptual-motor training for children who lack
proper coordination. These clinics provide exercises that
mimic the normal developmental movements a child should
have experienced to develop a flexible capacity for self-
control.

5. The most ambitious of the programs for the future
are the Research and Development Laboratories financed by
the USOE. There are 15 regional laboratories, nine
university-sponsored centers, and several related agencies in
operation now across the United States. All are engaged in
large-scale research and development as a systematic approach to the attainment of educational goals.

Two important products of these centers are: micro-
teaching, a method of in-service training for teachers to
improve classroom techniques through the use of video tape;
and the talking typewriter. The latter is a large, electric
typewriter with a screen attached equipped with programmed instruction. If the lesson is the letter "A," the letter "A"
is shown on the screen while the sound pronounces "A." The
child responds by striking the letter "A" on the keyboard. No
other key will strike except the letter "A."

Probably the most serious of all problems facing education is the rising cost. We simply must obtain more education
for the money expended. The USOE, in an effort to realize
full benefit from its investment in the Research and Development Program, has organized a coordinated research effort

involving 18 different states called "ES '70." Through the use of PPB (planning, programming, budgeting) and the techniques of systems analysis, "ES '70" has been given the following objectives:

1. Develop a learner-centered curriculum, relevant to roles students will play in adult life.
2. Individualize instruction for each student.
3. Utilize educational technology.
4. Establish suitable organizational patterns for schools.
5. Determine economic practicality within available resources.

Despite these promising developments, some serious problems of young people have hardly been touched upon. One of these is the plight of the student whose high anxiety level does not permit him to focus attention long enough to learn from any technique. A child unable to concentrate cannot absorb, retain, or organize knowledge. Until educators and researchers face squarely up to this fact, teachers and principals will continue to view innovations with skepticism. The quiet of the laboratory must be duplicated in the classroom.

It is quite possible that we must turn to the biochemist for the solution to this problem. David Krech, professor of psychology, University of California, Berkley, writes: The development of the mind of the child will come to rest in the knowledge and skills of the biochemist and pharmacologist and neurologist and psychologist and educator. And there will be a new expert abroad in the land—the psycho-neurobiochemeducator."[1]

The great transformation due in this decade which will improve the education of all children will be brought about by two novelties still in the incubation stage. They are individualized instruction and the involvement of the student in the selection of his own education.

Individualized or customized instruction has already

[1] Krech, David. "Psychoneurobiochemeducation." *Phi Delta Kappan.* Vol L, Number 1, March, 1969. p 370. Eighth and Union Ave., Bloomington, Indiana.

been accepted in principle. Educators acknowledge that humans differ in various kinds of intelligence, aptitudes, past learning experiences, personality, cultural and environmental history, and maturity development. The practice of exposing all children to the same curriculum and requiring comparable performance from each is *prima facie* unsound. In the past, individualized instruction has not been practical due to the cost and shortage of teachers, but the development of the teaching machine, married now to the computer, has changed the outlook. A report of the Congressional Sub-Committee on Economic Progress states: "It was pointed out that computers can provide lessons tailored to individual needs so that the student can control the speed of presentation in accordance with his own progress. The presentation can be in written form, through pictures, either moving or still, by voice or by various combinations of these. Likewise, the student responses can be made by typewriter keyboard, by pressing buttons or by simply pointing a wand at the tube."[2]

Although programmed instruction can develop rough categories of diversified curricula, once in operation they become relatively inflexible. A true symbiotic relationship between student and computer is possible in the future through further refinement of CAI (computer assisted instruction), since CAI will possess the following unique advantages:

1. *True Complete Diagnosis*—The computer can store many responses of the individual and then search these for stable patterns, characteristics, weak spots, and precise requirements of the moment.

2. *Evaluation*—The computer can accumulate extensive records of the student's responses, and furnish instant

---

[2] *Automation and Technology in Education.* A report of the Sub-Committee on Economic Progress of the Joint Economic Committee, Congress of the United States. August 1966. U.S. Government Printing Office, Washington, D.C.

evaluation of his immediate state of learning, not in comparison with others but with his own capabilities.

3. *Flexibility*—The computer can modify its own capabilities to meet changes and requirements of the student.

This does not envision the computer as the sole instructor, but as the teacher of basic skills and facts which are the foundation of education. Teachers will always be needed to supply warm, human understanding. Small group discussions must be available to advance social skills and interpersonal relationships. Lastly, much time must be allowed for independent study and writing. Only when forced to compose its own products does the human mind organize its knowledge and display its talent for creativity.

Most imperative of all, we must stop imposing education on children. Basically, this is the cause of their current restlessness. They see no relevance in what they are being taught because they cannot put it readily to use for their own benefit. It is an elementary fact of motivation that human beings, adults as well as children, need to know, "what's in it for me?" This is the very foundation of our system of free enterprise.

If the purpose of education is to prepare youth for adult responsibilities, it is only just that they be given the opportunity to choose the part in society they wish to play. Commensurate with their age and maturity level, they should be given a choice in selecting their own education with the full knowledge of the consequences, rewards, and responsibilities contingent upon their choice.

Youth wants most of all to be integrated into adult society. They need responsibilities and the privileges that go with such responsibility. The purpose of education should be to speed this process. Schools, with the co-operation of parents and the community, need to establish a whole system or hieirarchy of privileges that will accrue to students, dependent upon the education they choose and the diligence they apply to learning what they choose. No difference should be placed on the value of mastering bricklaying than upon the value of mastering medicine. These privileges will be roles and responsibilities open to them in adult society. Examples of such privileges would be driving permits, voting, opening charge accounts, marriage, ownership of property, and working permits. It must be made clear to them before they choose what immediate rewards they will be entitled to and what requirements will be necessary for them to obtain these rewards, as well as the responsibilities they must accept as a result of their choice. Only when they are able to decide their own futures will students find relevance in their education.

Index